48 HOURS
CA

C000245719

HOW TO ENJOY THE PERFECT SHORT BREAK IN 20 GREAT CITIES

The ❤INDEPENDENT

Mango Media
Miami
in collaboration with
The Independent

Independent Print Limited

Published by Mango Media, Inc.
www.mangomedia.us

This is a work of non-fiction adapted from articles and content by journalists of The Independent and published with permission.

48 HOURS IN...EUROPEAN CAPITALS *How to Enjoy the Perfect Short Break in 20 Great Cities*

ISBN: 978-1-63353-377-6

"Whether rediscovering old favourites or exploring new territory, enrich your experience with inside tips and under-the-radar information."

– Sophie Lam, Head of Travel

Table of Contents

PREFACE

Every Saturday in The Independent's award-winning Traveller section, our "48 hours" stories explore new and exciting city-break itineraries. Now, 25 years after the series was first launched, we've produced this book, designed to help you get the most from a visit to a selection of 20 European capitals.

The destinations we've focused on encompass well known and less- visited options, and offer travellers everything from dazzling architecture to world-class museums, designer shopping and historic landmarks. They're blessed with a range of accommodation options to suit every budget, restaurants for every taste, and bars and cafés that offer the chance to connect with local life. These are city breaks to tell your friends about; the sort of places that you'll want to revisit in order to discover more of their secrets.

We hope you enjoy planning your time away – and if you need further inspiration look out for more 48 hours ideas each week in The Independent.

Ben Ross, Travel Editor, The Independent

48 Hours in Amsterdam

The Dutch capital is back in full swing, thanks to the reopening of its top museum. Simon Calder finds cause for celebration.

TRAVEL ESSENTIALS
Touch down

Amsterdam Schiphol has better links from the UK than any other airport in the world, while frequent trains (€3.90 each way) from the airport take around 20 minutes to reach Centraal Station, where a decade of construction work is continuing. You can also reach Amsterdam in four hours from London St Pancras via Brussels with Eurostar (08432 186 186; eurostar.com). Stena Line (08445 762 762; stenaline.co.uk) offers "rail and sail" options from Harwich to the Hook of Holland, with train travel on to Amsterdam.

Get your bearings

Work started on the Canal Ring over 400 years ago to augment Amsterdam. It created the present-day framework for the city, which is basically a collection of islands divided by a ripple of concentric canals and united by bridges. The focus of the ring of semi-circular canals is Centraal Station, on the south bank of the broad IJ river. The main tourist office (00 31 20 702 6000; iamsterdam.com; open 9am-7pm daily) and public transport office (weekends 10am-6pm, weekdays 7am-9pm,) share a building opposite the station's main entrance. The original medieval city straggles south from here to scruffy Dam Square, presided over by the Royal Palace. West from here is the former Huguenot district of Jordaan; going south you reach the Museum Quarter.

Check in

The star property on the canal ring is Andaz at Prinsengracht 587 (00 31 20 523 1234; bit.ly/Andaz Library). A former humdrum city library has been transformed into a dramatic space with individually designed rooms, each rooted in Amsterdam tradition. There's no reception desk – just elegant staff equipped with iPads to check you in. An advance-purchase double starts at around €300, excluding breakfast.

If you are happy to stay slightly away from the centre, try the Lloyd Hotel & Cultural Embassy at Oostelijke Handelskade 34 (00 31 20 561 3636; lloydhotel.com) – once the embarkation point for emigrants. A one-star room with shared bathroom starts as low as €63 per double excluding breakfast; more luxurious options are available.

Should your main criterion be proximity to the great museums, Roemer Visscherstraat is the street to choose – with options including the rambling and friendly Owl Hotel at number 1 (00 31 20 618 9484; owl-hotel.nl). Doubles start at €112, including breakfast.

DAY ONE
Cultural morning

To see what can be done with a formidable collection of art, one third of a billion pounds and 10 years, arrive at opening time for the stunninng Rijksmuseum. A refurbishment that has taken most of the current millennium was completed in 2013, making it among the hottest tickets in Europe. Pre-book a €15 ticket at bit.ly/RijksT in order to dodge the queue.

Go straight up to the Gallery of Honour, where The Shooting Company of Captain Frans Banning Cocq – better known as Rembrandt's The Night Watch – is the only painting returned to its original position. Then explore the other galleries, where the history of the Netherlands is articulated in a fascinating range of objects and images.

Next, having pre-booked a specific time/date slot through bit.ly/VVGtickets, go to the front of the queue for the Van Gogh Museum (00 31 20 570 5200; 9am-6pm daily, Fridays to 10pm; €15). The tragic story of a fragile genius is portrayed through the world's finest collection of Van Gogh's work.

The Rijksmuseum

Window shopping

For independent stores aim for the Negen Straatjes, or Nine Streets – a district full of quirky enterprises. De Kaaskamer at Runstraat 7 sells the finest cheeses, while number 5, De Witte Tanden Winkel, sells dental accessories.

Lunch on the run

Café Papeneiland at the corner of the Prinsengracht and the Brouwersgracht (00 31 20 624 1989; papeneiland.nl) is an original "brown café", ideal for a snack with a coffee.

Take a hike

Close by are Amsterdam's Western Islands. From Haarlemmerplein walk north under the railway and wander through the villagey collaboration of canals, cottages, houseboats and bridges to the apartment block at the far end. Then head back, with Centraal Station as your beacon.

An aperitif

Amsterdam has more than its fair share of grand cafés, and the Café in the Waag at Nieuwmarkt 4 (00 31 20 422 7772; indewaag.nl) is one of the most spectacular, inside the oldest city gate.

Dining with the locals

Restaurant Anna at Warmoesstraat 111 (00 31 20 428 1111; restaurantanna.nl) has a chic interior and exquisite dishes such as truffle risotto followed by grilled scallops, which more than compensate for the Red Light District location. For €47.70 the chef will select four courses for you.

DAY TWO
Sunday morning: go to church

The Begijnhof, a flower-filled courtyard surrounded by gabled houses (begijnhof amsterdam.nl), was created for pious Catholic women who cared for the elderly and were themselves cared for by the Church. Today, it is a serene escape from the city outside – and home to one of the city's finest Protestant places of worship: the Engelse Kerk, which was adopted by Presbyterians in 1607. The pulpit has panels decorated by a young Piet Mondriaan. Sunday service is at 10.30am. Directly opposite stands the Begijnhofkapel, built in 1671. The doors are deliberately anonymous, but once inside it fans out to reveal an opulent interior in stark contrast to the "English church". Look for the stained-glass window dedicated to Holland's national poet, Joost van den Vondel; Sunday mass at 10am in Dutch and 11.15am in French.

Take a ride

Make your way to the northern exit of Centraal Station then pick your way across to the terminal for the IJ Buiksloterweg ferry.

Every few minutes, it sails across to Waterland – a serene area, steeped in tradition, with a new cinematic addition. Eye opened in 2012 with a vision to transform the city's waterfront (00 31 20 589 1400; eyefilm.nl; 10am-10pm). It includes four cinemas, and all kinds of tricks to entertain and enthral the eye.

Out to brunch

What really draws the eye – and the visitors to this side of the IJ – is the museum's Eye Bar Restaurant (00 31 20 589 1402; eyebarrestaurant.nl), with a wide-screen view across the river.

Coffee and croissants are served 10am-noon daily, followed by a lunch menu.

A walk in the park

Hortus Botanicus (00 31 20 625 9021; dehortus.nl) began as an herb garden in 1638. Soon, the Dutch East India Company started bringing back strange and exotic plants from around the world, and the place blossomed into a small but delightful botanical garden. Its greenhouses include some plants that are extinct in the wild. There is also a pleasant courtyard cafe. The garden is open 10am-5pm at weekends, €8.50.

Amsterdam Botanical Gardens

Icing on the cake

If you are flying home, take a last look at treasures from the Rijksmueum at Schiphol airport, "airside" between D and E piers; open daily 7am-8pm; free.

48 Hours in Berlin

Uncover culture and history in the German capital, says Chris Leadbeater.

TRAVEL ESSENTIALS
Touch down

Berlin's much-delayed new airport, Brandenburg, isn't scheduled to open until 2015. The two airports it was designed to replace will continue to handle flights until then. Tegel lies five miles northwest of the centre. The Jet Express Bus TXL runs from the airport to the central Alexanderplatz in 30 to 40 minutes, for €2.30. Taxis take 20 minutes, for €25.

Schönefeld airport is 11 miles east of the city and handles a wider range of flights. The airport has a dedicated station. Airport Express trains to Alexanderplatz take 25 minutes. S-Bahn trains S9 and S45 do the same. The one-way fare is €3.20. Taxis cost about €45.

Get your bearings

All public transport from the airports – and within the city – is part of the Berliner Verkehrsbetriebe system (bvg.de). Single tickets in central zones (A and B) are €2.30, valid for two hours. A one-day ticket (A, B) is €6.30.

Though no longer divided by its infamous Cold War wall, Berlin still has marked eastern and western halves. The former, in districts such as Mitte and Prenzlauer Berg, has most of the landmarks, museums and nightlife. The latter still has fine shops and sights.

Two loosely parallel lines of water, the Spree river and Landwehr Canal, frame the centre. Visit Berlin (00 49 30 2500 2333; visitberlin.com) has an office on Pariser Platz (9.30am-7pm). Its two-day WelcomeCard (€18.50) covers transport and museum discounts.

Check in

A funky dark-decor hotel in Mitte at Torstrasse 136, Mani does doubles from €77, room only (00 49 30 530 280 80; hotel-mani.com). To the east, in Friedrichshain, at Landsberger Allee 106, Andel's Hotel (00 49 30 453 0530; vi-hotels.com/andels-berlin) has doubles for €120, room only – and a 14th-floor bar. A five-star dame in an enviable location at Unter den Linden 77, the Hotel Adlon has doubles from €220, room only (00 49 30 22 610; kempinski.com).

DAY ONE
Take a hike

Start at the junction of Friedrichstrasse and Unter den Linden. The latter is Berlin's main avenue, and has regained its pomp since reunification in 1989. Stroll west, to Pariser Platz, to Brandenburg Gate, a postcard moment. This 18th-century triumphal arch became a totem of Cold War schism as the Wall ran right in front of it. From here, trace the old line of the Wall south on Ebertstrasse, pausing at the Memorial to the Murdered Jews of Europe, where 2,711 concrete blocks remember the Holocaust. Below (entrance at Cora- Berliner Strasse 1), an exhibition gives sombre context (00 49 30263 9430; stiftung-denkmal.de; 10am-8pm Tuesday-Sunday; free).

Continue south on Ebertstrasse into Potsdamer Platz, down Stresemannstrasse. Take the second left, halting at Niederkirchnerstrasse 8, for the Topography of Terror, a museum amid the ashes of the former SS and Gestapo HQ (00 49 30 2545 0950; topographie.de; 10am-8pm; free).

Return to the Brandenburg Gate. Opposite lies the Tiergarten, Germany's second-biggest city park. It offers 520 acres of leafy calm. The Victory Column (Siegessäule) is a monument to 19th- century Prussian military might. Barack Obama spoke here in 2008.

Brandenburg Gate

Lunch on the run

On the top edge of the Tiergarten at Scheidemanstrasse 1, the Berlin Pavillon (00 49 30 3980 0880; berlin-pavillon.de) is of note, partly for its lunches (a hearty beef sandwich is €11) and for its view of the Reichstag, Germany's stately glass-domed parliament.

Window shopping

To the south of the Tiergarten at Tauentzienstrasse 21-24, the KaDeWe department store has long been a fixture of west Berlin (00 49 30 21210; kadewe.de). Nowadays it has rivals in the east of the city, especially on store-lined Friedrich-strasse, where Galeries Lafayette, at Nos 76 to 78, offers gilded competition (0049 30 209480; galerieslafayette.de). For more idiosyncratic retail options, hop over to the north of Mitte, where Mulackstrasse, in particular, provides designer swagger.

Starstyling Berlin, at No 4 (00 49 30 9700 5182; starstyling.net) does bright modern garb, and shares its address with Rug Star (00 49 30 6666 8315; rug-star.com), which takes a chic approach to carpets. Lala Berlin, at No 7 (0049 30 2576 2924; lalaberlin.com) delivers cutting-edge couture.

An aperitif

Elsewhere in Mitte, Clärchens Ballhaus, at Auguststrasse 24 (00 49 30 282 9295; ballhaus.de), is a 1913 dance hall – where the Roaring Twenties still echo around its elegant, if semi-dilapidated rooms. The outdoor beer garden pours out giant German lagers.

Dining with the locals

Gastro choices abound in Mitte. The restaurant at Mani (see Check In) continues the hotel's offbeat theme, mixing French and Israeli fare into the likes of its Jerusalem artichoke soufflé.

Katz Orange, at Bergstrasse 22 (00 49 30 9832 08430; katzorange.com), occupies a converted brewery – and offers saltmarsh lamb or €25.

Rutz, at Chausseestrasse 8 (00 49 30 2462 8760; rutz-weinbar.de), revels in a wine list that runs to 800 varieties as it serves ox shoulder for €24.

Or flit over to ever-trendy Kreuzberg, where Volt, at Paul-Lincke-Ufer 21 (00 49 30 6107 4033; restaurant-volt.de), does risotto with scallops in a former electricity substation.

DAY TWO
Sunday morning: go to church

Perched on Lustgarten park, the Berliner Dom (00 49 30 2026 9136; berlinerdom.de) is a resurrection tale. It was bombed in 1944, then rebuilt to its 1905 design, and fully reopened in 1993. It is open for visits for €7 – although there is, of course, no charge for its main Sunday mass, at 10am.

It is not, however, Berlin's most striking church. That's west Berlin's Kaiser-Wilhelm-Gedächtniskirche (00 49 30 218 5023; gedaechtniskirche-berlin.de; 9am-7pm; Sunday mass 10am), on Breitscheidplatz. Shattered by Allied fire in 1943, its shell has been left as an anti-war statement, a 1960s chapel sprouting from the ruins.

Berlin Cathedral on Museum Island

Cultural morning

Adjacent to the Dom, Museumsinsel (Museum Island) is Berlin's prime cultural pocket. Five key institutions all come under the Berlin State Museums banner (00 49 30 2664 24242; smb.museum), and deserve lengthy exploration. The Pergamonmuseum (Am Kupfergraben; daily 10am-6pm; €13) hosts antiquities excavated in Turkey, Greece and Iraq in the 19th century. The Alte Nationalgalerie (Bodestrasse 1-3; daily 10am-6pm, closed Monday, Thursday 10am-10pm; €8) houses works by such German greats as Carl Blechen and Caspar David Friedrich, as well as pieces by Monet and Manet. And the Bode Museum (Am Kupfergraben 1; daily 10am-6pm except Thursday (10am-10pm); €8) is a treasure trove of Byzantine art. A three-day Museum Pass (€24) gives entry to the whole "island".

Out to brunch

Monsieur Vuong is a modern Vietnamese restaurant that's popular with the locals at Alte Schönhauser Strasse 46, in Mitte (00 49 30 9929 6924; monsieurvuong.de). Try the chicken-heavy glass noodle salad Mekong.

Take a ride

Berlin is big and difficult to absorb, but you can see a lot on two wheels. Fat Tire Bike Tours – based at Panoramastrasse 1a, (00 49 30 2404 7991; fattirebiketours.com/berlin) – runs a variety of themed jaunts for €24 each. The "Raw Tour: Berlin Exposed" lasts five hours and nine miles, and dissects vibrant districts, such as Kreuzberg, that have bloomed in the past 20 years.

Icing on the cake

Go back in time at the East Side Gallery, the largest remaining section of the Berlin Wall that stood from 1961 to 1989 (eastsidegallery.com). Stretching for a mile along Mühlen-strasse, this de-fanged symbol of oppression is preserved as an artwork, with 106 striking murals.

48 Hours in Brussels

Belgium's capital is easy to reach and explore, and full of gastronomic and architectural treats. By Cathy Packe.

TRAVEL ESSENTIALS
Touch down

Eurostar (08432 186 186; eurostar.com) has nine daily trains to Brussels Midi station, taking less than two hours from London St Pancras. Alternatively, Brussels airport lies 11km to the north-east of the city. Trains depart frequently from the airport station and stop at both Midi and Central stations; the journey takes 20 to 30 minutes, and costs €7.60 one way.

Get your bearings

Central Brussels consists of the lower town, whose focal point is the Grand Place, and the upper town containing the royal palace, parliament and other state institutions. The tourist office is in the lower town at 2-4 Rue Royale (00 32 2 563 6399; biponline.be) and opens 10am-6pm daily. Here you can buy a Brussels Card, (brusselscard.be) affording entry to more than 30 of the city's museums, unlimited travel by bus, metro and tram, and discounts at a number of shops, restaurants and attractions. The card costs €24 for 24 hours or €34 for 48 hours. Central Brussels is enclosed within the inner ring road, outside which are a number of suburbs, including the European quarter where all the main EU buildings are located. Two official languages are spoken in Brussels, French and Flemish; street names are given here in their French version.

The Grand Palace in Brussels

Check in

Odette en Ville is a chic boutique hotel tucked away at 25 Rue du Chatelain, a quiet street off Avenue Louise (00 32 2 640 2626; chez-odette.com) within easy reach of trams to the city centre; doubles from €250, with an extra €25 for breakfast.

The friendly, family-run Vintage Hotel at Rue Dejoncker 45 (00 32 2 533 9980; vintagehotel.be) is a recent addition to the hotel scene, decorated in homage to the 1960s and 70s. Doubles from €120, including breakfast.

In the Marolles district, the pleasant, well-located Hotel Galia at 15-16 Place du Jeu de Balle (00 32 2 502 4243; hotelgalia.com) has doubles from €75, including breakfast.

DAY ONE
Take a ride

Like many other cities, Brussels has installed ranks of bicycles for residents and visitors to hire for short periods; given the compact nature of the city, they provide an ideal way to explore. The Villo bikes (villo.be) are yellow, and can be found in 180 locations. Buy a one-day card for €1.60 at any terminal with a card reader, then follow the instructions to take your bike from the stand. The first half-hour is free, the next costs €0.50, and charges increase the longer you keep the bike.

Line of rental bicycles at a Villo station

Window shopping

For the traditional Brussels souvenir, chocolate, head to the Place du Grand Sablon, where all the tastiest names – Leonidas, Wittamer, Neuhaus and, most luxurious, Pierre Marcolini – are found. Every weekend a market held in front of the church sells bric-a-brac and antiques.

For design head to Rue Antoine Dansaert, which has become the centre of the Brussels fashion industry. Among the stores to seek out is Stijl at number 74, showcasing a number of cutting-edge designers. Normal shopping hours are 10am-7pm.

Lunch on the run

At the bottom end of Rue Dansaert is the original branch of the now world-wide chain, Le Pain Quotidien, serving soups, sandwiches and salads, a tiny place that is often crammed with people. An alternative is the bustling Via on the Quai à la Houille.

Cultural afternoon

Brussels was the adopted home of René Magritte, who came to study here at the age of 18, and remained in the city for much of his life. More than 200 of his paintings, drawings and sculptures are on display in the Magritte Museum, in a striking neo-classical building on Place Royale (00 32 2 508 3211; musee-magritte- museum.be; open 10am-5pm daily except Monday; Tuesdays and Wednesdays to 8pm; admission €8).

To find out about Magritte in more domestic surroundings, take tram number 94 from outside the museum to the suburb of Jette and visit the house at 135 Rue Esseghem (00 32 2 428 2626; magrittemuseum.be) where he lived for more than two decades with his wife Georgette, and where he had a studio. The walls of the sitting room are painted in the sky blue colour that appears in many of Magritte's works, and many features of the rooms, including doors, windows and a fireplace, feature in his paintings. The house opens from Wednesday to Sunday 10am-6pm, admission €7.

An aperitif

The Flat at 12 Rue de la Pépinière, is a sort of home-from-home – at least in the sense that this is a bar where you can drink in rooms furnished like an apartment – so if you like to sup your cocktails in the kitchen or the bathroom, this is the place to go. If you prefer a Belgian beer, L'Ultime Atome, in the lively surroundings of Rue Saint-Boniface, is always a good choice.

Dining with the locals

The Bozar Brasserie (00 32 2 503 00 00; bozar.be) is a popular spot to eat, so reservations are recommended. The chef is David Martin, well-known in the city for his Michelin-starred restaurant, La Paix, in the Brussels suburb of Anderlecht. His new brasserie is on Rue Ravenstein in the extravagant Bozar building, formerly the Palais des Beaux-Arts. It opens noon-11pm daily.

DAY TWO
Sunday morning: go to church

Perched on a small hill, the gothic Cathedral of St Michael and St Gudule would once have dominated the medieval skyline. Building began in the early 13th century and was finished over the course of 300 years. Restoration efforts show off the beautiful stone carvings and elaborate wooden pulpit inside.

Out to brunch

Brunch has become very popular in Brussels; one of the most copious spreads is offered in the café at the Bla Bla Gallery on Rue des Capucins (00 32 2 503 5918; blablagallery.com). Stick to traditional breakfast dishes and pay €15.50 for your meal, or add in a hot dish, salad and dessert for €22.50.

Take a hike

This tour explores Brussels' eclectic mix of architecture. The Art Nouveau movement began here, and several fine buildings from this period remain. Start at Merode metro station and look first at the Maison Cauchie, a block away to your left. This was designed by Paul Cauchie, an important Art Nouveau architect, and the facade of the tall, thin building is covered with sgraffiti: figures which are carved into the stone, but appear to have been painted. If you are visiting on the first weekend of the month you will be able to get inside; the house opens 10am-1pm and 2-5.30pm, admission €5.

From here, walk across the Cinquantenaire Park, laid out in 1880 to celebrate the 50th anniversary of Belgian independence. On either side of the main avenue are museums, devoted to Art and History and to the Army. In the far corner of the park, you'll find a small pavilion designed by Victor Horta, one of the main exponents of the Art Nouveau movement. Leave the park by the exit nearest to the Pavilion and head down to Square Ambiorix. On the north side is one of the most striking buildings in Brussels, the house built for the artist Georges Saint-Cyr, with elaborate tracery and wrought ironwork.

Further down on Avenue Palmerston is Horta's Hotel van Eetvelde, whose façade, with its industrial-style steel and glass exterior, was revolutionary when it was built in 1895. Walk south and west, through Brussels Park, designed in the 18th century in a formal

French style, with the elegant facades of the Royal Palace and the Belgian Parliament facing each other. Finish at another Art Nouveau building, once the Old England department store, now the Musical Instruments Museum (00 32 2 545 0130; mim.be; 9.30am-5pm Tuesday-Friday, from 10am at weekends; €8).

Take a view

The Rooftop Café inside the Musical Instruments Museum has a great view over the city centre. For a different perspective, take metro line 6 to Heysel and exit at the Atomium, a silvery representation of an iron molecule – a landmark on the Brussels skyline and also the best place from which to get a view of the city. Five of its nine spheres are open to the public, and the panoramic view can be seen from the highest one. Others contain a permanent exhibition about the 1958 World's Fair, for which the Atomium was built, as well as temporary exhibits. Open 10am-6pm, €11.

A walk in the park

Stretching out beyond the Atomium is an area of parkland. At its heart is the Parc de Laeken, a pleasant space which contains the residence of the royal family as well as a Japanese pagoda and Chinese pavilion. Several metro stations along the edge of the park are on line 6, which will take you back to the city centre.

48 Hours in Budapest

Music, culture and innovative nightlife combine to create the perfect break in the Hungarian capital. By Charles Hebbert.

DAY ONE
Touch down

Taxis are available from the Fotaxi kiosks outside Budapest's airport (00 36 1 222 2222; fotaxi.eu; from 5100 forint /£15); or catch the Airport Shuttle bus (00 36 1 296 8555; airport shuttle.hu) which will drop you at your address from 3200Ft (£8.85).

Alternatively, catch the train from the station next to Terminal 1, where no-frills airlines arrive, to Nyugati Station, a couple of metro stops from the city centre. You can buy tickets (365Ft/£1.20) at the Tourinform desks in the terminals. If your flight arrives at Terminal 2B, you'll need to catch bus 200E (320Ft/85p) to reach it.

Get your bearings

The main axis of the city is the River Danube, flowing south towards the Black Sea, which is crossed by a series of bridges. On the western side is hilly Buda, the former seat of government with the Royal Palace and the old Castle District, which has a more sedate pace. Pest, on the eastern side, is the flat, bustling commercial centre. Radiating out from the Belvaros, the touristy inner city, are grand boulevards such as Andrássy út that proclaim the confidence of the city in its late 19th-century golden age.

The tourist office is at Suto utca 2, off Deak ter (square), where the three metro lines converge at Deak Ferenc ter station. You can buy single tickets (320Ft/85p) for public transport or in books of 10 (2,800Ft/£9.30) from metro stations. Remember to validate each one. Alternatively, buy a Budapest Card (7,500Ft/£20.75 for 48hrs), which covers public transport (but not the Siklo funicular), entrance to museums and restaurant discounts.

Check in

The Continental Hotel Zara at Dohany utca 42-44 (00 36 1 815 1070; continentalhotelzara.com) offers four-star comfort and a roof-top pool. Note its glorious Art Nouveau façade preserved from the former Hungarian baths. Doubles start at €85, including breakfast. The Star Inn Hotel Budapest Centrum, Dessewffy utca 36 (00 36 1 472 2020; starinnhotels.com) is good value at €59, room only. By far the best budget option is Homemade at Terez korut 22 (00 36 1 302 2103; homemadehostel.com – original, quirky and brilliantly run; doubles from 11,000Ft (£31), room only.

Take a ride

Hop aboard the number 2 tram at the northern end of its run, Jászai Mari tér, by the Margit hid (bridge), and enjoy the perfect introduction to the city as you ride down the Pest side of the river.

On Kossuth ter, you pass the imposing neo-Gothic parliament and the grand Museum of Ethnography (neprajz.hu; 1300Ft/£3.60; 10am-6pm daily except Monday), which has a fascinating display on Hungarian folk art. You are then swept along the embankment with a grandstand view of the Castle District on the Buda side.

Passing under the Lanchid (also known as the Szechenyi Chain Bridge), the first bridge to be built between Buda and Pest, you head on down to Fovam ter, the stop for the Central Market Hall (Nagycsarnok). The tram goes on to the Palace of Arts (00 36 1 555 3300; mupa.hu), the cultural centre down the river that boasts one of the finest concert halls in Europe.

Window shopping

The smells of paprika, salami and fresh vegetables fill the air in the magnificent wrought-iron, turn-of-the-century Central Market Hall (open Saturday 6am-2pm; Monday 6am-4pm, Tuesday-Friday 6am-6pm). The stalls set up down the right-hand side are aimed at tourists, so avoid them if you want to shop with the locals.

Szechenyi Chain Bridge

Lunch on the run

Behind the market, the friendly Borbirosag restaurant at Csarnok ter 5 (00 36 1 219 0902; borbirosag.com), serves delicious Hungarian-style tapas and fuller meals: the duck breast and red cabbage is 2,650Ft/£7.30) is the pick of the salads. The "Wine Court" also serves excellent Hungarian wines – it is worth exploring the country's lesser known indigenous wine varieties such as the white Furmint or red Kadarka.

Cultural afternoon

The Applied Arts Museum (imm.hu; 10am–6pm daily except Monday; 1,000Ft/£2.75) by the Corvin negyed station in southern Pest is a flamboyant concoction in a style that typifies Hungarian Art Nouveau. One of the exotic turn-of-the-century designs by the Hungarian architect Odon Lechner, it blends Hungarian and Turkic ornamentation outside, while the pure white interior looks like something out of a Mogul palace. The permanent display includes such delights as a wonderful Art Nouveau wooden and gold clock.

An aperitif

The city is endowed with grand coffee houses, such as the sophisticated Central at Karolyi Mihaly utca 9. Stop for a coffee as you watch locals continue the tradition of writers and artists of the late 19th century.

As the evening draws on, you will discover the vibrant nightlife of Budapest in the "ruin garden" bars. Kazinczy utca has several, the most stable venue in this fluid scene being the Szimplakert at number 14. This former stove factory now accommodates a colourful jumble of outdoor and indoor bars. Spritzers are the in- drink – ask for a froccs (pronounced "frurch").

Dining with the locals

One of Budapest's best restaurants is the Bock bisztro at Erzsebet korut 43-49 (00 36 1 321 0340; bockbisztro.hu; closed Sunday), a small restaurant that serves traditional Hungarian dishes with a modern spin, such as chicken paprika with cottage cheese dumplings; the wine here is just as important as the food.

Standards are equally high at the elegant Var: a Speiz at Hess Andras ter 6 (00 36 1 488 7416; varaspeiz.hu) in the Castle District. The menu includes a "breadcrumb parade", where dishes are priced from 2,800Ft (£7.70) – wiener schnitzel will never taste the same again.

DAY TWO
Sunday morning: go to church

The neo-gothic style Matyas Church in the Castle District has a flamboyantly painted interior – you can avoid the 990Ft (£2.75) entry fee by attending Sunday mass at 8.30am or the grander 10am service with a choir and which is celebrated in Latin.

Take a view

In the shadow of Matyas Church's spire, the Fishermen's Bastion (Halaszbastya) is a mock rampart, whose seven turrets symbolise the Hungarian tribes that came to Europe. It offers a sweeping view of the Danube and Pest.

Old Fishermen's Bastion, Budapest

Take a hike

From Matyas Church, head west to Ruszwurm, a touristy but delightful coffee house that has been at Szentharomsag utca 7 for almost 200 years. Of the many museums in the district, you could choose the Golden Eagle Pharmacy museum at Tarnok utca 18 (10.30am–5.30pm daily except Monday; semmelweis.museum.hu; 700Ft/£1.95), which has a wonderful collection of questionable medical tools and cures.

Walking south, you come to the Royal Palace, which houses the Hungarian National Gallery (mng.hu; 10am–6pm daily except Monday; 1,400Ft/ £3.85). This boasts some of Hungary's finest artists, such as Csontvary, the 19th-century visionary whom Picasso admired, and Rippl-Rónai with his masterly Art Nouveau canvasses.

From here, take the Siklo funicular (840Ft/£2.80) down to the river bank and cross the Lanchid to the superbly restored Art Nouveau Gresham Palace on Szechenyi ter for a coffee in the glass-roofed lobby of the Four Seasons hotel (00 36 1 268 6000; fourseasons.com/Budapest).

Out to brunch

Continue along the riverside to Peppers restaurant at the Marriott Hotel at Apaczai Csere Janos utca 4 (00 36 1 737 7377;

peppers.hu) in Pest. It has a superb buffet (noon-3pm on Sunday) of Hungarian classics and international dishes: all you can drink and eat for 9,500Ft (£26) per person; children under six go free and can enjoy craft activities in a supervised playroom.

A walk in the park

Catch the yellow metro line 1 from Vorosmarty ter close to the Marriott and get off at Hosok ter for the verdant expanses of Varosliget, the City Park, which is studded with museums and playgrounds. Behind Hosok tere and its parade of great Hungarian leaders is a rowing lake that turns into an ice rink in winter, with its backdrop of the fairy-tale Vajdahunyad Castle.

The icing on the cake

The Szechenyi thermal bath (00 36 1 363 3210; szechenyi-bath.com; entry from 4,600Ft/£12.70; daily 6am-10pm, steam rooms close at 7pm) is also located in the park. This is that unmissable Budapest spa moment. Besides its open-air pool with chess players, it also has an outdoor whirlpool plus steam rooms and cold plunges inside – 16 pools in all. You'll need to hire a swimming cap to swim in the big outdoor pool.

48 Hours in Copenhagen

The Danish capital is an enticing gourmet destination. Chris Leadbeater gets a taste for it.

TRAVEL ESSENTIALS
Touch down

Copenhagen's main airport, Kastrup (cph.dk), lies five miles south of the centre. The city operates a zonal transport system, so the three-zone trip to the centre costs Dkr36 (£4) whether you travel by train (dsb.dk), which takes 12 minutes to reach the Hovedbanegard rail terminus; metro (m.dk), which takes 15 minutes to get to Norreport station; or bus No 5A (moviatrafik.dk), which takes about 30 minutes to reach the Hovedbanegard. Taxis take around 20 minutes and cost about Dkr250 (£29).

Get your bearings

Almost at the easternmost point of Denmark, Copenhagen preens on the east coast of the vast Zealand island, separated from Sweden by the 15-mile width of the Oresund strait. The city is split into districts by myriad canals and waterways – of which Indre By (the historic core), bohemian Christianshavn and gentrifying Vesterbro detain most visitors.

Metro (two lines), S-train (seven lines; dsb.dk/s-tog) and bus services dissect a city that is easily explored on foot. All are covered by transport tickets sold at stations and bus stops. A basic ticket – Dkr24 (£3) – is valid for one hour in the two central travel zones.

City Passes cost Dkr75 (£8.50) for 24 hours; Dkr190 (£22) for 72 hours. The main Visitor Centre (00 45 70 22 24 42; visitcopenhagen.com) is at Vesterbrogade 4A – open daily from 9am-6pm (except Sunday, 9am-2pm). The Copenhagen Card (transport and entry to 75 attractions) costs Dkr299 (£34) for 24 hours, Dkr449 (£52) for 48 hours.

Check in

The Axel Hotel Guldsmeden (00 45 33 31 32 66; hotelgulds-meden.dk) is a small four-star at Helgolandsgade 7-11 that contributes to Vesterbro's trendy vibe with a cocktail bar in its lobby. Double rooms start at Dkr995 (£114), without breakfast.

Another four-star haven of peace amid the eateries of Nyhavn dock (at No 71), is the 71 Nyhavn Hotel (00 45 33 43 62 00; 71nyhavnhotel.dk). Doubles from Dkr1,099 (£126), room only.

A five-star icon at Kongens Nytorv 34, all ballrooms and bling, is the Hotel D'Angleterre (00 45 33 12 00 95; dangleterre.dk), where you can blow the budget with a double for Dkr5,500 (£631), room only.

DAY ONE
Take a hike

Begin by ambling through Slotsholmen, the island that is a key component of Indre By, divided from Christianshavn by the channel of the Inderhavnen (Inner Harbour). Here, the Black Diamond – an angular extension to the Royal Danish Library, completed in 1999 – is the star of the waterfront. The library complex, at Soren Kierke-gaards Plads 1 (0045 33 474 747; kb.dk), is open daily except Sunday, with one-hour tours on Saturdays at 3pm for Dkr40 (£5). Follow Christians Brygge to the south-eastern corner of Slotsholmen. Stop for a bite at Kayak Bar at Borskaj 12 (00 45 30 49 86 20; kayakrepublic.dk) or continue north-west along Borsgade, noting the Borsen – the oldest stock exchange in Denmark, dating to 1619 – which is remarkable for its spire of four entwined dragons. Further on, the Christiansborg Palace hosts the Danish parliament.

Copenhagen's Christiansborg Palace

Window shopping

Running between Kongens Nytorv and Radhuspladsen squares, Stroget is the main shopping street, pedestrianised for a mile (stroget-kobenhavn.dk). The Royal Copenhagen store at Amagertorv 6 (00 45 33 13 71 81; royalcopenhagen.com) is the flagship of the Danish brand which has been making porcelain since 1775. Sostrene Grenes at Amagertorv 24 (00 45 36 97 81 10; grenes.dk) sells quirky discount homeware. BoConcept at Gammel Kongevej 29A in Vesterbro, is a Danish design firm that fits into the cool district with sleek seats and crafted chairs (00 45 33 26 87 87; boconcept.dk).

Lunch on the run

Next to the Royal Copenhagen store, also at Amagertorv 6, the Royal Smushi Café deals in open flat-bread sandwiches such as the Baronessens Luksus with its piled salmon, shrimp and asparagus for Dkr145 (£17) (00 45 33 12 11 22; royalsmushicafe.dk).

Take a ride

Canal Tours Copenhagen (00 45 32 66 00 00; stromma.dk) offers a one-hour "Grand Tour" of the Inderhavnen port that departs from the dock at Gammel Strand, meandering past landmarks such as the Little Mermaid – the bronze statue of Hans Christian Andersen's creation, perched just off the Langelinie promenade in the Osterbro district. At least four tours an hour; Dkr75 (£8.50).

An aperitif

Dip into Vesterbro at Lidkoeb, a chic bar at Vesterbrogade 72B, where the Valkyrie cocktail mixes bourbon, lemon and apple for Dkr100 (£11) (00 45 33 11 20 10; lidkoeb.dk).

Dining with the locals

Vesterbro's meat-packing past is celebrated at BioMio at Halmtorvet 19 (00 45 33 31 20 00; biomio.dk), where chefs cook in a kitchen in the middle of the room. Noma, on the Christianshavn flank of Inderhavnen, at Strandgade 93 (00 45 32 96 32 97; noma.dk), has regularly been voted the world's top restaurant. Its three-course menu, for Dkr1500 (£172), includes dishes such as roast turbot with celeriac. Reservations essential.

Rather less formal, the address is in the name at dockside eatery Nyhavn 37 (00 45 33 15 70 76; nyhavn37.dk), where the 37's burger is Dkr139 (£16).

DAY TWO
Sunday morning: go to church

A glorious baroque temple, the Vor Frelsers Kirke (Our Saviour's Church) thrusts a black-and-gold spire into the sky above Christianshavn, at Sankt Annae Gade 29. Consecrated in 1695, it is open daily 11am-3.30pm, with Sunday mass at 10.30am. But the selling point is the tower view, open daily, entry Dkr40 (£4.50) (00 45 32 54 68 83; www.vorfrelserskirke.dk).

Walk in the park

On the south-east side of Christianshavn, Christiania (00 45 32 95 65 07; christiania.org) is the self-proclaimed "autonomous neighbourhood" that was founded on an old military base in 1971. With graffiti-daubed homes, it looks stuck in the hippie era, but offers a snapshot of commune life, and beers for Dkr25 (£3) at Café Nemoland (Fabriksomradet 52; 00 45 32 95 89 31; nemoland.dk).

Out to brunch

Back in modern Christianshavn, Café Oven Vande sits beside a canal at Overgaden Ovenvandet 44. It serves a fish-heavy ocean sandwich for Dkr110 (£12.50), and glimpses of houseboats on the water (00 45 32 95 96 02; cafeovenvande.dk).

Carlsberg Glyptotek, Copenhagen

Cultural afternoon

The Nikolaj Kunsthal hosts art shows in the shell of the 13th-century St Nicholas's church, at Nikolaj Plads 10 (00 45 33 18 17 80; kunsthal.dk). It is open daily except Monday, admission free. Elsewhere in Indre By, the Nationalmuseet at Ny Vestergade 10 (00 45 33 13 44 11; natmus.dk/en), charts the history of Denmark in detail. It is open daily except Monday, free entry.

Nearby at Dantes Plads 7, the Ny Carlsberg Glyptotek is an art treasure trove with a wealth of sculpture by Rodin, open daily except Monday; Dkr75 (£9) (00 45 33 41 81 41; glyptoteket.com).

Icing on the cake

Copenhagen is hugely proud of the Tivoli – the enclave of ornate gardens and thrill rides that has lit up its map at Vesterbrogade 3, since 1843 (00 45 33 15 10 01; tivoli.dk). Open daily; admission Dkr95 (£11). Rides cost extra – from about Dkr25 (£3).

48 Hours in Dublin

Write your own chapter in this most literary of cities, says Susan Griffith.

TRAVEL ESSENTIALS
Touch down

The airport is 12km north of the centre. The frequent Aircoach (aircoach.ie) costs €7 one way, €12 return to Upper O'Connell St, Grafton Street and Merrion Square North. Dublin Bus's 747 Airlink (dublinbus.ie) to Connolly and Heuston railway stations costs €6 one way, €10 return. City bus 16A departs every 20 minutes (exact fare, €3.05). By sea, Irish Ferries (08181 300 400; irishferries.com) has fast ferries and conventional ships to Dublin from Holyhead; from Stena Line (0844 770 7070; stenaline.co.uk) runs a seasonal high-speed catamaran to Dun Laoghaire (see "Icing on the cake"), where you can plug into the city's Dart light-rail system.

Get your bearings

The River Liffey bisects the city horizontally. Orient yourself by the named foot and road bridges, the most central of which is busy O'Connell Bridge. The heart of the city is demarcated by Trinity College, St Stephen's Green, Christ Church Cathedral and Parnell Square, with Temple Bar at the centre. The Dublin Tourism Centre on Suffolk Street (00 353 1 437 0969; visitdublin.com) opens 9am-5.30pm daily except Sundays (10.30am-3pm). The bus information office at 59 Upper O'Connell Street (00 353 1 873 4222; dublinbus.ie) provides a guide to key routes.

Check in

The Westbury Hotel (00 353 1 679 1122; doylecollection.com) offers stylish rooms and a location that could not be more central. Doubles without breakfast start at €235. The Townhouse bed and breakfast on the north side at 47/48 Lower Gardiner Street (00 353

1 878 8808; townhouseofdublin.com) occupies two restored Georgian houses, one of which belonged to Lafcadio Hearn, the 19th-century writer on Japan, which explains the Japanese garden. Doubles from €56, with breakfast.

Among the many hostels, Kinlay House near Christ Church (00 353 1 679 6644; kinlaydublin.ie) has dorm beds from €15 with decent breakfasts.

DAY ONE
Cultural morning

In this most literary of cities, make libraries your theme. Sequestered behind St Patrick's Cathedral, Marsh's Library (marshlibrary.ie) has been a public library since 1701 (the first in Ireland) though today's scholars are no longer locked into three cages at the back to prevent theft. This under-visited gem is open weekdays 9.30am-1pm and 2pm-5pm, Saturdays 10am-1pm, closed Tuesdays; €2.50.

The Chester Beatty Library displays illuminated manuscripts from Asia and the Middle East, and astonishing early papyrus fragments of the Bible. Open 10am-5pm from Tues-Sat, 1-5pm Sun; free. Also free is the National Library of Ireland at 2 Kildare Street (nli.ie); open daily, hours vary.

Lunch on the run

George's Street Market is great for lunch and people-watching. Groups of teenage girls concoct frozen yoghurt desserts at innovative Yogism. Elegant ladies with slim ankles sip espressos. Order a €5 lamb burger at the Honest to Goodness Café Bakery or slide into a communal bench at Urban Picnic for an Asian or Mediterranean-influenced dish.

Window shopping

In the George's Street Arcade eclectic stalls sell records, retro clothes, modish jewellery and second-hand books of Irish poetry (georgesstreetarcade.ie). The market opens at 9am daily (noon on Sundays) and closes at 6.30pm (8pm Thursdays). A short walk away, Lucy's Lounge, a thrift shop at 11 Upper Fownes Street, rotates a wacky stock of fashion and accessories.

George's Street Arcade, Dublin

An aperitif

The whimsical out-of-the-way The Cake Café at 62 Pleasants Place (00 353 1 478 9394; thecakecafe.ie) serves prosecco and elder-flower cocktails and fino sherry with olives for €7 in tiny premises and a leafy arcaded courtyard; open till 5.30pm on Saturdays, 8pm Tuesday to Friday.

Apart from such frivolities, Dublin is a one-aperitif town – though locals would never besmirch the good name of Guinness with that fancy description. The traditional Dublin pub, with polished mahogany and cut-glass mirrors is a thing of beauty. Go to buzzing Neary's behind the Gaiety Theatre for the banter, to Mulligan's for an unreconstructed old-world atmosphere, to The Long Hall for its diversity of regulars or to The Brazen Head, a stronghold of Irish nationalism judging from the portraits.

Dining with the locals

The Celtic Tiger era left Dublin with a selection of impressive dining options such as the Camden Kitchen (00 353 1 476 0125; camdenkitchen.ie) just around the corner from The Cake Café (see An aperitif), and Hugo's at 6 Merrion Row (00 353 1 676 5955; hugos.ie) with contemporary dishes such as grilled artichoke salad and tamarind-glazed salmon.

At La Cave Wine Bar, at 28 South Anne Street (00 353 1 679 4409; lacavewinebar.com), the subterranean location, "bordello red" decor and Latin music manages to create an intimate yet casual atmosphere. If you are prepared to leave by 8pm, two courses cost €17.

DAY TWO
Sunday morning: take a view

As the morning sky brightens over the River Liffey, stroll downstream on the north side towards the newly renovated Docklands. Just before the Sean O'Casey Bridge is a disquieting reminder in bronze of the Great Famine of 1845-1852. With their backs turned on Ireland, five straggling figures and an emaciated dog look towards the sea, with emigration their only hope. The modern view is of the stunning Samuel Beckett Bridge and the port beyond.

A walk in the park

Just 10 minutes' walk from the River Liffey is the fine Georgian Merrion Square, where well-to-do families lived (and where a soup kitchen was set up during the famine). Famous residents included the Wildes (Oscar's father was a prominent surgeon) and W B Yeats at number 82. In the centre is a railed-in pleasure ground, adorned with gas lamps of Old Dublin, a tent-shaped war memorial and sculptures. The most arresting is of Oscar Wilde, draped languidly over a boulder in the corner nearest his childhood home.

Out to brunch

Presiding over Grafton Street, Bewley's Oriental Café (bewleys.com) is one of Dublin's charming clichés, a monument to respectability, purveyor of fine coffee and a €9.60 full Irish breakfast at any time after 9am on Sundays (8am on other days).

Take a hike

At a time when cemeteries were exclusively Protestant, the nationalist hero Daniel O'Connell established non-denominational Glasnevin Cemetery in 1832. It has monumental sculptures, mature sequoia, yew and oak, and the remains of more than a million souls. The tombs of the famous cluster round the entrance on Finglas Road (accessible by bus 40 or 140), from the grandiose 50m round tower above a sunken crypt for "The Liberator" O'Connell, to the modest headstone of Ireland's early president, Eamon de Valera. The daily 2.30pm tour (€10) provides a fascinating insight into the who's who of Irish history. Wandering to the more neglected corners reveals epitaphs that record the poignant loss of children in large impoverished Irish families.

Grave of Irish revolutionary Michael Collins, Glasnevin Cemetery

Icing on the cake

Jump on a Dart commuter train to Dun Laoghaire and inside half an hour you can be striding out on the mile-long East Pier, enjoying marvellous views across Dublin Bay and watching shags dive for fish.

Walking south along the shore about the same distance brings you to quaint Sandycove and the Martello Tower made famous in the first chapter of Ulysses. Back in the city, find your way to the unfashionable Smithfield area to hear informal Irish music at the Cobblestone pub at 77 North King Street (00 353 1 872 1799).

48 Hours in Edinburgh

Head to the Scottish capital for its Old and New Towns – and some Harry Potter lore. By Simon Calder.

TRAVEL ESSENTIALS
Touch down

Edinburgh's Waverley station is tucked between the city's Old and New Towns. Edinburgh airport, seven miles west, has flights from across the UK. The Airlink 100 bus (0131 555 6363; flyby-bus.com) departs from outside the terminal at least every 10 minutes for the half-hour journey to Waverley station via Haymarket station; £4 single/£7 return. The Edinburgh Pass (edinburgh.org/pass) starts working from the airport – it includes a return trip on the Airlink bus, as well as admission to more than 30 attractions; a two-day pass costs £40.

Get your bearings

Edinburgh is a collection of villages that clings to the skirts of the Castle, perched atop a volcanic plug. The ancient centre is the Old Town, around the spine of the Royal Mile – which changes its name several times as it runs down from the castle. The south side is a mix of grand institutions and student haunts, while to the north stands the handsome 18th-century New Town. Edinburgh's window on the maritime world is Leith, on the Firth of Forth. The main tourist office is at 3 Princes Street (0845 2255 121; edinburgh.org), part of the Waverley station complex. It is open daily.

Check in

The last great Victorian railway hotel to be completed was the North British, which opened in 1902 on Princes Street and is now known as the Balmoral (0131 556 2414; thebalmoralhotel.com). A double with breakfast costs around £300. The rack rate for suite 552, where J K Rowling completed Harry Potter and the Deathly Hallows is £1,275 a night. When she finished on 11 January 2007, the world's most successful writer signed an antique Florentine bust of Hermes – god of travel – that happened to be in the room. It has been preserved there in a glass case. Mere mortals who are hurrying for their trains at Waverley should note that the hotel's clock is deliberately set fast to encourage tardy travellers not to dawdle.

Le Monde at 16 George Street (0131 270 3900; lemondehotel.co.uk) brings the world to Edinburgh, with individually designed and named rooms from Paris and Milan to Havana and Shanghai. Doubles start at around £175, including breakfast.

The best-located budget hotel is the Ibis Edinburgh Centre, just off the Royal Mile at 6 Hunter Square (0131 240 7000; ibishotel.com). Advance booking doubles start at £83, excluding breakfast.

DAY ONE
Take a hike

The Royal Mile is the collective name for the straggle of streets leading west up to the Castle. Start at the Queen's official residence when she's in Scotland, Holyroodhouse, open daily (0131 556 5100; bit.ly/HolyEdi; admission £11.30).

When power was devolved back to Scotland after three centuries, the nation built a new and eccentric power base near the foot of the Royal Mile. Free guided tours of the labyrinthine interior of the Scottish Parliament operate 11am to 5.30pm on Saturdays, Mondays and Fridays (0131 348 5200; scottish.parliament.uk).

The Museum of Edinburgh in historic Huntly House tells the capital's story, while the Canongate Tolbooth opposite contains the People's Story Museum. Continue past St Giles' Cathedral and follow signs to Lady Stair's House, occupied by the Writers' Museum. Here, you learn "the happiest lot on earth is to be born a Scotsman". All three open 10am to 5pm and noon to 5pm Sundays at festival time; free.

Take a view

Camera Obscura at 549 Castlehill offers an optical feast: the city and its skyline projected on to a concave dish, on which you can pick out pedestrians along the Royal Mile. There's also a mirror maze (0131 226 3709; camera-obscura.co.uk; 9.30am to 9pm; £12.95).

Lunch on the run

The café in the crypt of St Giles' Cathedral (0131 225 5147) offers stovies (slowly stewed meat, potato and onion, £6.50), alongside a daily Scottish special. Afterwards, take the short cut from the café into the handsome body of the church (0131 225 9442; www.stgilescathedral.org.uk; 9am to 5pm Saturdays, 1 to 5pm Sundays, 9am to 7pm other days).

National Gallery of Scotland

Cultural afternoon

The Neoclassical Scottish National Gallery includes works by Rubens, Gauguin and Cézanne, and the museum's motif: Sir Henry Raeburn's Skating Minister (0131 624 6200; nationalgalleries.org; 10am to 5pm daily, Thursday to 7pm; free).

Across in the Old Town, the National Museum of Scotland on Chambers Street (0300 123 6789; nms.ac.uk; 10am to 5pm daily; free) tells the story of the nation. The highlight is the Grand Gallery, a vast and elegant space newly liberated from a century of clutter.

An aperitif

"The birthplace of Harry Potter" is how the Elephant House at 21 George IV Bridge (0131 220 5355; elephanthouse.biz) bills itself: J K Rowling began her writing career in the big, bright back room of this rambling café. As the sun sinks over the castle, you can sink a single malt, Scottish beer or a sauvignon.

Dining with the locals

Either stay on at the Elephant House for haggis, neeps and tatties, or head across to the New Town. The Dome at 14 George Street (0131 624 8624; thedomeedinburgh.com) was formerly the Commercial Bank of Scotland. Starters include haggis in filo pastry (£7.50). The signature main is an 8oz Scottish fillet steak (£29.50).

DAY TWO
Sunday morning: go to church

Princes Street Gardens separates the Old and New Towns. Descend by the steps near the west end of Princes Street to the atmospheric old churchyard of St Cuthbert's, strewn with ancient tombstones. Cross the footbridge over the railway and follow the path that winds around Castle Rock. Take Granny Green's Steps down to the former execution site of Grassmarket and find the northern entrance to Greyfriars Kirk – the city's first post- Reformation church. The churchyard is full of dramatic memorials, while the Kirk itself (0131 226 5429; greyfriarskirk.com) has an elegant, austere interior. Visitors welcome at Sunday services (11am in English, 12.30pm in Gaelic).

Walk in the park

Calton Hill rises 450ft above sea level. It hosts the National Monument, an ambitious attempt to replicate the Parthenon in the "Athens of the North": work stopped after a dozen Doric columns had been completed. Close by, you can climb the 170 steps of the Nelson Monument (10am to 6pm daily; from 1pm on Mondays; £3) for fine views across the city, the Firth of Forth and a swathe of southern Scotland.

Window shopping

Edinburgh sustains plenty of independent shops, with a cluster of galleries and boutiques along Victoria Street. On Leith Walk, Valvona & Crolla at 19 Elm Row (0131 556 6066; valvonacrolla.co.uk) is a divine delicatessen offering all kinds of Mediterranean aromas and flavours – including a dozen varieties of olive oil.

Out to brunch

Valvona & Crolla also has a restaurant at the rear; open 10.30am to 3.30pm Sundays, longer hours other days. Sip strong coffee and feast on Italian home cooking.

Take a ride

Bus 22 will take you to the Ocean Terminal, location for the Royal Yacht Britannia – a true floating gin palace aboard which the Queen and Prince Philip entertained dignitaries (0131 555 5566; royal-yachtbritannia.co.uk; 9.30am to 4.30pm; £12.75). It provides a fascinating glimpse into regal circles –and the monarch's tastes.

Take tea on deck and enjoy views of Fife.

Icing on the cake

Edinburgh Castle

Finish at the high and mighty Castle. The stronghold of Scotland has served as royal residence and military headquarters, and is now the nation's leading paid-for attraction (0131 225 9846; edinburgh-castle.gov.uk; 9.30am to 6pm; £16). From the battlements, you can appreciate the spectacular contours and architecture of this multi-faceted city.

48 Hours in Helsinki

Water is the key to the appeal of the Finnish capital, says Chris Leadbeater.

TRAVEL ESSENTIALS
Touch down

The city's main airport, Helsinki-Vantaa (00 358 200 14636; hel-sinki-vantaa.fi), is 12 miles north of the centre. Bus 615 visits both terminals every 15 minutes, and costs €4.50 for a 30-minute ride that drops you in Rautatientori, outside the city's art nouveau rail station. The Finnair City Bus traces an identical route in 20 minutes, for €6.20. Taxis ask €20-€30.

Get your bearings

Helsinki lies on Finland's south coast, hard against the Gulf of Finland – the easternmost arm of the Baltic Sea. Water is key to its appeal: while the hub of the city sits on terra firma, the landmass is laced with lakes and channels – and several of Helsinki's big sights perch on islands just off-shore, notably the 18th-century sea fortress of Suomenlinna. The centre fans out north of the shoreline, a mixture of the pragmatic and the pretty – and the fruit of two distinct eras.

Helsinki was founded as a trading post in 1550 by Gustav I of Sweden – in a period when the Finns lay under the yoke of their west-erly neighbours – but did not enter its glory years until 1808 when Russia conquered the region and remodelled the city as a sibling to St Petersburg. This latter influence is visible in Senaatintori (Senate Square), where a statue of Tsar Alexander II, Finland's ruler between 1855 and 1881, surveys what was once his realm.

The metro largely caters for commuters and is of little use to tourists, but buses, trams and local ferries are plentiful. Single tickets for all four services (Helsinki Regional Transport: 00 358 9 4766 4000; hsl.fi) cost €2 if bought in advance from metro stations or tram stops, and cover unlimited journeys in a one-hour window. A one-day pass costs €8.

Tickets are also available at the tourist information office at Pohjoisesplanadi 19 (00 358 9 3101 3300; visithelsinki.fi, and also visitfinland.com) – as is the Helsinki Card (helsinkiexpert.com). This covers all public transport and most museums, priced €39 for 24 hours, €51 for 48, €72 for 72. However, with the city compact enough to be explored on foot, the card is good value only if you visit at least three institutions.

Check in

A short stroll from the museums at Pohjoinen Rautatiekatu 23, Hotel Helka is a gently stylish three-star, with a sauna and doubles from €124, including breakfast (00 358 9 613 580; helka.fi). The four-star Hotel Torni, at Yrjonkatu 26 (00 358 20 123 4604; soko-shotels.fi), is an Art Deco dame that dates to 1928; doubles from €114, with breakfast. The Hotel Kamp at Pohjoisesplanadi 29 (00 358 9 576 111; hotelkamp.com) is a gilded 1887 five-star, where local boy Sibelius used to drink. Doubles from €224.

DAY ONE
Take a hike

Market Square or Kauppatori

Alive with people on the edge of the harbour, Kauppatori (Market Square) gives notice that Helsinki is still a busy port, its stalls overlooking docks where ferries pull in from Stockholm and St Petersburg. However, the city's softer side quickly takes over in the form of the Esplanadi – a manicured walkway that offers hints of Paris as it flows uphill – part Jardin des Tuileries in its leafy café culture, part Champs Elysées in the two chic avenues (Pohjoisesplanadi and Etelaesplanadi) that flank it.

Follow the Esplanadi to the top and turn right on to Mannerheimintie, then right again to move on to Aleksanterinkatu. The city's main shopping drag is a further echo of the Russian era, bearing the name of Alexander I (Tsar 1801- 1825) as it spears east into Senaatintori.

Window shopping

Aleksanterinkatu is dotted with the usual international names and chain brands – but brandishes a symbol of retail tradition at number 52, where Stockmann (00 358 9 1211; stockmann.com) does seven storeys of department store finesse dating back to 1930.

Inquisitive visitors should skip south to the Punavuori district, the heart of Helsinki's design scene. Nou Design at Uudenmaankatu 2 (00 358 50 60081; nounoudesign.fi), dishes up some really cool kitchenware, and Design Forum at Erottajankatu 7 (00 358 9 6220 8130; designforumshop.fi), offers products of myriad talented Finns. The Classic Audio, at Iso Roobertinkatu 44 (00 358 500 550 054; classicaudio.fi), sums up the district's ethos by dispensing vintage stereo equipment and old radios.

Lunch on the run

Just off the Esplanadi at Kluuvikatu 3, Fazer (00 358 20 729 6702; fazer.fi) is a hallowed landmark: an 1891 coffee salon. Indulge your sweet tooth with its many pastries and cakes, or try the signature Fazer chocolate tea.

Cultural afternoon

Helsinki's major museums are gathered in a cluster immediately north of the centre. The Kansallismuseo (the National Museum of Finland), at Mannerheimintie 34 (00 358 9 4050 9544; kansallismuseo.fi; Tuesday 11am-8pm, Wednesday to Sunday 11am-6pm, Monday closed; €8), is a faux-Gothic castle in which the history

of the country from the Stone Age onwards is dissected – folk tradi-
tions, Sami culture and a "throne room" containing one of the regal
chairs that seated the 19th century tsar overlords.

Metres away at Mannerheiminaukio 2, Kiasma (the Museum of
Contemporary Art) is a stark pile of concrete and glass that acts as
Helsinki's modern art showcase (00 358 9 1733 6501; kiasma.fi;
10am-5pm daily except Monday, with late opening on Wednesday
and Thursday to 8.30pm, and Friday to 10pm; €10).

Finland's National Gallery, Ateneum, at Kaivokatu 2 (00 358 9
1733 6401; ateneum.fi), houses the titans of Finnish art – Akseli-
Gallen Kallela, Helene Schjerfbeck – plus pieces by Van Gogh and Gauguin. It opens 11am-5pm at weekends, other days 10am-6pm,
Wednesday and Thursday to 8pm, closed Monday; €12.

An aperitif

Hop back to Punavuori and sip a beer amid the hip young things
at Café Bar 9, at Uudenmaankatu 9 (00 358 9 621 4059; bar9.net).
There is nothing especially striking about its mildly gloomy interior –
small tables and a long bar against the back wall – but the atmosphere
is lively.

Dining with the locals

Havis at Etelaranta 16 (00 358 9 6128 5800; royalravin-
tolat.com/havis) is an upmarket fish restaurant that occupies a prime
slice of Helsinki's harbourfront. The signature dish is the chargrilled
perch for €30.

Slightly less pricey, Bar Kanava, at Kanavaranta 7 (00 358 9 6128
5520; royalravintolat.com/kanavabar), serves roasted Finnish sir-
loin with a chorizo salad for €24.

DAY TWO
Sunday morning: take a ride

From Kauppatori, pick up the ferry that sails to Suomenlinna
every 20 minutes (taking 12 minutes to do so). This colossal stronghold was founded by the Swedes in 1748, and is so large it stretches
across eight close-knit islands. Even 250 years on, it bristles with de-
fensive might, tall ramparts and cannons threatening the sea.

Nonetheless, it failed in its moment of truth: when Russia invaded in 1808, Sweden surrendered it with barely a struggle.

Take note of the Kirkkopuisto church, which hails from the Russian era. Its dome doubles as a lighthouse whose beams are visible from the mainland at dusk.

War Museum at Suomenlinna

Out to brunch

Slotted into the fortress's outer walls next to the ferry jetty, Panimo ("Brewery") serves up solid staples such as Finnish salmon soup and spicy lamb sausages with vegetable mash, as well as fine house beers (00 358 9 228 5030; panimo.com).

Go to church

The Tuomiokirkko (the Lutheran cathedral), Helsinki's most dramatic structure, rises on a low hillock above Senaatintori (00 358 9 2340 6120; www.helsinginseurakunnat.fi/tuomiokirkko). Open daily, it is a fantasy in white – and also something of a reverse- Tardis. From the outside, it appears vast and ornate, gold crosses crowning green domes. Within, it is oddly compact and austere – a statue of Martin Luther one of the few adornments. He glares into the distance at the rival Uspenski Cathedral, a red-brick Orthodox bastion that, with its cupolas and icons, could not look more Russian. Open noon-

3pm on Sundays, 9.30am-4pm on other days (00 358 207 220 683; ort.fi/helsinki).

A walk in the park

Laid out in the 1830s as a strolling enclave for the Russian aristocracy, Kaivopuisto park exudes a breezy nobility as it spreads out at the southern tip of the centre, within sight of the Baltic. A statue at its western corner, Odotus (Expectation) – a bronze figure of a mother gazing worriedly at the horizon – is far less cloying a concept than it sounds.

The icing on the cake

Round off your stay at the Hotel Torni, whose 14th (and top) floor is given over to the Ateljee Bar (00 358 9 4336 6340; ateljee-bar.fi) – a tiny watering hole filled with evening drinkers and character in an equal measure. The cocktails are hardly cheap (though Champagne is €8 a glass on Monday and Tuesday) but the view over city rooftops justifies the expense.

48 Hours in Lisbon

From cutting-edge design to high-end cuisine, there's plenty to lure visitors to the Portuguese capital. By Sophie Lam.

TRAVEL ESSENTIALS
Touch down

The airport is 7km north-east of the city. The easiest way into town is on the Aerobus (carris.pt), which departs every 20 minutes between 7am-11pm, stopping at a dozen destinations, and terminating at Cais do Sodré train station. A single fare is €3.50, taking 25-30 minutes. The ticket is valid for the rest of the day on the city's bus network. A taxi is marginally faster, costing around €15.

Get your bearings

Cultural, cutting edge and full of character: the Portuguese capital lays on centuries of history, then throws in barrios that bubble with bohemian flair and forward-thinking projects such as the transformation of neglected buildings by large-scale urban artworks (cargocollective.com/crono).

Like Rome, Lisbon is set on seven hills, but pre-dates the Italian capital by about 400 years. The city shoots up either side of the flat Baixa district, which channels down towards the broad, Tagus river. An epic earthquake destroyed much of the city (and around 35,000 lives) in 1755. Lisbon was then redesigned by the then-Prime Minister, the Marques de Pombal – most notably Baixa, as a district of broad avenues and spacious squares. Moorish quarters, or barrios, still mark out the hills: the Bairro Alto (nightlife) and Chiado (shopping) on the west, and multi-cultural Mouraria, ancient Alfama and Castelo, with the 12th-century Sao Jorge Castle, to the east.

View from Santa Justa elevator in Baxia

The transport system comprises a four-line metro (metrolisboa.pt), buses (carris.pt) and idiosyncratic trams, many of them more than 100 years old. The easiest way to get around is with a one-day travel card (€4.60; first buy a rechargeable card for €0.50). The Lisbon Card (€18.50 for 24 hours) is available from the tourist office on Praca do Comercio (00 351 210 312 7000; askmelisboa.com; daily 9am-8pm).

Check in

Four Seasons Ritz Lisbon at 88 Rua Rodrigo da Fonseca (00 351 21 381 1400; fourseasons.com/lisbon) lives up to expectation. Huge rooms overlooking Parque Eduardo VII and old-fashioned glamour set the scene, while a swanky spa and high-hitting restaurant, Varanda, keep things current. Doubles from €360, including breakfast.

Design junkies should check into Fontana Park, providing sharp lines and dark hues in a converted metalworks at 2 Rua Engenheiro Vieira da Silva (00 351 21 041 0600; fontanaparkhotel.com).

Doubles from €90, B&B.

Lisbon frequently tops worldwide hostel polls; Traveller's House has won the "Hoscars" for the last four years. Located at 89 Rua Augusta (00 351 21 011 5922; travellershouse.com), it offers dorm beds for €20 and doubles from €54, both with breakfast and lashings of style.

DAY ONE
Take a hike

Start at Parque Eduardo VII, a sloping ribbon of green named after the English king who visited in 1902 that ends at Praca Marques de Pombal, with its bronze statue of the Portuguese prime minister. Continue south down Avenida da Liberdade, the 90m-wide boulevard modelled on Paris, lined with the likes of Prada and Armani and shaded by a canopy of trees. The road ends at Praca dos Restauradores, a touristy congregation of eateries.

Continue south to Praca Dom Pedro IV, also known as Rossio, a large square dedicated to Pedro IV of Portugal, the first ruler of the empire of Brazil – note the iconic black and white wave mosaic floor, also seen beside Rio de Janeiro's beaches.

Cross to the square's eastern periphery and continue south down Rua Augusta, a busy, pedestrianised thoroughfare lined with old-fashioned shops. Head under the arch built to commemorate the 1755 earthquake and finish at the Praca do Comercio, an enormous square that ends at the mighty Tagus.

Take a view

Switch back up Rua do Ouro and stop at the 45m-tall iron monolith that is the Elevador de Santa Justa. Built by an apprentice of Gustave Eiffel in 1902 to connect Baixa with the lofty Largo do Carmo, the lift and viaduct now double as a tourist attraction (00 351 21 361 3054; carris.pt) offering elevated views of the city.

Returns €5, or use your travel card. Open daily 7am-9pm.

Lunch on the run

Jose Avillez's CV takes in stints with Ferran Adrià and Alain Ducasse and a Michelin star at Lisbon-lux restaurant Tavares. Now, in Chiado, the young chef has created an informal address of his own with Cantinho do Avillez at 7 Rua dos Duques de Braganca (00 351 21 199 2369; cantinhodoavillez.pt). Contemporary Portuguese dishes such as steak sandwiches, Alentejo-style black pork (both

€8.50) and scallops with avocado (€8.25) are served in a perfectly pitched atmosphere of laid-back sophistication.

Window shopping

Chiado is Lisbon's elegant and easy-going shopping district. On the pedestrianised Rua do Carmo H&M, Footlocker and a bustling mini-mall jostle for space with stand-out stalwarts such as Luvaria Ulisses at number 87a (00 351 21 342 0295; luvariaulisses.com), which has been selling hand-made gloves since 1925. Around the corner at 7 Rua Garrett, Paris em Lisboa is a wood-fronted shop dating back to 1888, specialising in linen (00 351 21 346 8885).

An aperitif

Shoot skywards at the Tivoli Lisboa hotel, 185 Avenida Liberdade (00 351 21 319 8900; tivolihotels.com) to the rooftop, where you emerge from the lift at the Euro-chic Sky Bar. The sunset views are breathtaking, encompassing the pink-tinged city as it shelves into Baixa and down towards the Tagus. An Absolut Vanilla in the Sky cocktail costs €11.

Dining with the locals

Seek out one of the superior little restaurants in the Bairro Alto. A Cataplana at Rue do Diario de Noticias (00 351 21 342 2993) is typical – just 20 places with a smattering of kisch and elegant tiles. Here you can have a meaty or fishy meal for two with a carafe of robust wine.

DAY TWO
Sunday morning: out to brunch

Deli Delux at 8 Avenida Infante D Henrique (00 351 21 886 2070; delidelux.pt) is a bourgeois food emporium with a small café that spills onto a terrace, sometimes right up against docked cruise ships. Nevertheless, it's a popular spot and offers fresh continental breakfast for €9.50, or €13 if you add scrambled eggs with Serrano ham, smoked salmon or asparagus (10am-4pm at weekends).

Go to church

Continue along the Tagus and weave up through the sinuous roads of Alfama, beneath washing-bedecked windows, to the Se, Largo da Se (00 351 21 887 6628), the much-modified 12th-century cathedral built by the first king of Portugal. The two imposing bell towers give it the impression of a medieval fortress and indeed the interior is a little austere. However, a mother-of-pearl safe contains the relics of the city's patron saint, St Vincent and sections of the mosque that it was built over have now been uncovered. Open daily 10am-7pm, free (though visiting the cloisters costs €2.50).

Cultural morning

From the Se, wind uphill to the Castelo district and the Sao Jorge Castle. This is where Lisbon was first occupied during the Iron Age. Pass under the Arch of Sao Jorge and wander the pretty residential streets inside Castelo's walls (sections of which date back to Roman times), then into the Castle (00 351 21 8800 620; castelosaojorge.pt; daily 9am-6pm; €7.50). Explore the ruins of the 14th- to 16th-century royal residence, the 10 towers and camera obscura, then make for the main square, with its old cannons and impressive city views.

Take a ride

Head back in the direction of the Se; just before you round the corner to the cathedral, hop aboard tram number 28 (carris.pt). Built of wood and chrome in the early 20th century, the yellow cars clunk their way down past the cathedral, swerving down vertiginous roads and dipping down into Baixa before clambering their way back up to the Bairro Alto. Watch your valuables on board.

A walk in the park

Get off the tram at Santa Caterina and walk up Rua do Seculo, through the romantic Praca do Principe Real and across to the Botanical Gardens. The gardens (00 351 21 392 1893) at Rua da Escola Politecnica are accessed via an avenue of palm trees. Enter a haven of shady walkways, beds planted with 10,000 exotic trees, plants and shrubs and a large pond full of ducks and lily pads. Open 10am-6pm on Sundays, 9am-6pm other days; €2.

The icing on the cake

From Cais do Sodre station board a train to Cascais. The 40-minute trip takes you on a scenic journey along the Tagus towards the Atlantic. Landmarks along the way look familiar, even to the first-time visitor – the 25 April suspension bridge is a doppelganger for the Golden Gate Bridge (and built by the same company) and Cristo Rei could pass for Rio de Janeiro's Christ the Redeemer. You'll also pass the fairytale Belem Tower, languishing just offshore, as well as the enormous gothic-renaissance Jeronimos Monastery. The train pulls into the pretty little seaside resort of Cascais, with sandy coves ideal for soaking up the sun, or sunset.

Belem Tower on the Tagus River

48 Hours in Luxembourg

The Grand Duchy's capital offers grand distractions, says William Cook.

TRAVEL ESSENTIALS
Touch down

Findel airport is 6km east of Luxembourg City. Board bus 9 or 16 at the airport: both leave every 10 minutes and take half an hour (fare €2) to reach the central train station. A taxi costs about €25.

Get your bearings

A bizarre, beguiling blend of metropolis and market town, the Grand Duchy's compact capital is one of Europe's best-kept secrets. Though better known as a financial centre, it has a thriving cultural scene and its picturesque streets are never overrun by tourists.

Perched on a rocky plateau, protected by a deep ravine, Luxembourg has a breathtaking setting. The historic centre is encircled by the river Alzette and its tributary, the Pétrusse.

The modern districts of Gare and Bonnevoie are on the south side of the river, linked to the centre by several vertiginous bridges.

Hidden in the river valley are the quaint old villages of Grund and Clausen. Kirchberg, to the north, used to be the site of the city's fortress; today it's the new cultural and commercial district.

The national tourist office (00 352 4282 821; ont.lu) is located in the train station (open weekdays 9am-6.30pm, weekends noon-6pm). Staff sell two-day Luxembourg Cards (€19) that offer free public transport, plus free or reduced admission to attractions. You can also buy this pass at the city tourist office on Place Guillaume II (00 352 222 809; lcto.lu), open 9am-7pm daily (except 10am- 6pm Sundays).

Check in

Le Place d'Armes at 18 Place d'Armes (00 352 27 47 37; hotel-leplacedarmes.com) is a five-star hotel converted from a row of 18th-century houses. It is a debonair blend of old and new with a popular brasserie. Doubles from €320, room only.

Parc Beaux Arts at 1 Rue Sigefroi (00 352 26 86 761; parcbeauxarts.lu) is a good four-star, housed in an antique town-house with contemporary furniture and striking modern art, 10 suites and a convivial restaurant. Doubles from €169 including breakfast.

Luxembourg also has a splendid Youth Hostel at 2 Rue du Fort Olisy (00 352 2627 6640; youthhostels.lu). It's in a peaceful riverside spot, surrounded by woods and fields. You'd never guess the city centre was a short walk away. A bunk bed in a six-berth dorm costs €23.50pp, with breakfast, plus €3 for non-members.

Double rooms cost €5 more per person.

DAY ONE
Take a hike...

...through the historic centre. Collect your sightseeing bumph from the helpful tourist office on Place Guillaume II, then cross the city's most handsome, historic square and into Rue du Marché aux Herbes. Stop to admire the ornate Grand Ducal Palace – a 16th- century edifice and the first city hall. Walk right up to the main gates and gawp at the splendid sentries. If you're lucky, you might see the Grand Duke. Head right, downhill on Rue du St Esprit.

Take a view

Built on several steep hills, divided by perilous gorges, Luxembourg is full of stunning vistas. One of the best is from the terrace of the quirky Musée d'Histoire de la Ville de Luxembourg at 14 Rue du St-Esprit (00 352 4796 4500; mhvl.lu). The ride up to the terrace, in a glass lift, is a panoramic treat in itself. Open 10am to 6pm daily except Monday, Thursday to 8pm. Entry €5; free Thursdays 6-8pm.

Grand Ducal Palace

Take a ride

From Rue du St-Esprit, cross the giddy viaduct, then stroll south past the chain stores of the lively, unpretentious Avenue de la Gare until you reach the train station. For a DIY bus tour, board the No 16 (00 352 2465 2465; mobiliteit.lu; fare €1.50), alight at Philharmonie, Luxembourg's beautiful modern concert hall at 1 Place de l'Europe (00 352 26 02 27 1; philharmonie.lu). The European Parliament is just across the road. Hop back on the bus as far as Royal to take you back into the centre.

Lunch on the run

Luxembourg is a city relatively free of sightseers, with lots of locals working in the heart of town, and it has plenty of good-value, good-quality lunch options. A La Soupe at 9 Rue Chimay (00 352 2620 2047; alasoupe.net) is a sleek, bustling café serving healthy stews and sandwiches. (Try their minestrone with white beans and parmesan.) A soup or salad and dessert, plus a hot or soft drink, costs €9.90. It opens 7am to 8.30pm daily except Sunday.

Window shopping

La Grand-Rue is Luxembourg's smartest shopping street with lots of upscale designers, including Max Mara and Gérard Darel, as well as smaller boutiques. For chocolates, visit Namur at 27 Rue des Capucins (00 352 223 408; namur.lu). A Luxembourg institution since 1863, this chic confiseur is heaven for anyone with a sweet tooth. A box of its exquisite home-made chocolates costs anything from €7 to €78.

An aperitif

Right next door to Namur is Le Vis-à-Vis at 2 Rue Beaumont (00 352 460 326), an old-fashioned Luxembourgeois bar thick with cigarette smoke. (You're still allowed to smoke in bars in Luxembourg, so long as people aren't eating.) Try a glass of the local lager, Diekirch. It's open from early morning until 1am Monday to Saturday, 3-8pm Sunday. If the tobacco smog inside gets too much, you can take your drinks outside.

Dining with the locals

In virtually any other European capital the Bistro de la Presse at 24 Rue de Marché aux Herbes (00 352 46 66 69; bistrodelapresse.lu) would be a tacky, overpriced tourist trap. Here in homely Luxembourg it's an unpretentious restaurant, serving hearty regional staples, with a bar propped up by convivial locals rather than camera-clicking sightseers. A vast, nourishing tureen of bouneschlupp (green bean soup with sausage) costs €13.50. Half a litre of wine to wash it down will set you back €7.

DAY TWO
Sunday morning: go to church

Luxembourg's Notre Dame (00 352 222 9701; cathedrale.lu) hardly qualifies as one of Europe's great cathedrals, but its modest proportions and humble ambience are part of its appeal. An odd melange of Gothic and Renaissance architecture, mainly built in the 17th century, it feels like a living, working church. Services every Sunday at 9am, 10.30am and noon.

Out to brunch

Most eateries remain shut on Sunday mornings, but the café at Chocolate House, 20 Rue du Marché aux Herbes (00 352 2626 2006;

chocobonn.lu), serves a continental breakfast of croissants, ham and cheese and you can order a glass of champagne to go with it. Downstairs is the chocolatier, with all sorts of creations (try the chocolate chilli) to eat in or take away. It's open 10am-8pm Sunday, from 9am Saturdays and 8am on weekdays.

Medieval street, Luxembourg

Cultural afternoon

Luxembourg's cultural kingpin is the Musée d'Art Moderne at 3 Park Dräi Eechelen (00 352 453 7851; mudam.lu; open Saturday to Monday 11am-6pm, to 8pm Wednesday to Friday; €5). Built within the ruined walls of an old fortress, it's not just a challenging forum, but an artwork in its own right. Designed by IM Pei, this graceful new building completes his "European Trilogy", alongside his Louvre extension in Paris and the German Historical Museum in Berlin.

More traditional tastes are met by the National Museum of History and Art on Marché-aux-Poissons (00 352 479 3301; mnha.lu; 10am-6pm daily except Monday, to 8pm Thursday; €5). The fine art includes works by Cézanne, Picasso and Magritte, but the highlight for British visitors is a pair of Turner watercolours depicting Luxembourg's old town and the dramatic landscape.

Icing on the cake

Luxembourg used to be one of the most fortified cities in Europe, and you can still walk along its ruined battlements. Start at the Bock Casemates, a labyrinth of tunnels built to withstand the fiercest siege, and follow the signposts for the Wenzel Path down the valley, across the river Alzette and through the Neumünster Abbey.

Follow the Pétrusse, the Alzette's tributary, along the leafy Vallée de la Pétrusse. The path rises into the city beneath the spectacular Adolphe bridge. The end of the Wenzel Path brings you to the pretty Municipal Park. The park's main landmark is Villa Vauban (00 352 4796 4900; villavauban.lu). This 19th-century mansion is now a smart art museum.

Out to brunch

The classic Spanish snack for elevenses is chocolate y churros. The churros are like crisp and sugary doughnuts. Those served at Muniz at Calatrava 3 are among the best.

A walk in the park

Take Metro Line 2 to Retiro station. The Parque del Buen Retiro is Madrid's most important expanse of green. This 350-acre park is the city's weekend (and weekday) playground, where joggers pound the winding paths, friends gather at cafés and couples sit on the steps of weighty monuments. The curving colonnade that tips its hat to 19th-century monarch Alfonso XIII is particularly striking – while El Angel Caído, a statue by Spanish sculptor Ricardo Bellver, depicting Lucifer tumbling from heaven, injects an unexpected note of darkness into this pastoral enclave.

The icing on the cake

Retreat to the centre, and the fabled Chocolatería San Ginés, a Madrid institution at Pasadizo de San Ginés 5 (00 34 91 365 6546) that has been selling gloopy hot chocolate with churros since 1894. Go elbow-to-elbow with fellow churro-dippers amid the long mirrors and green velvet seats, and marvel at the fact that, though the Chocolatería is open 24 hours a day, the queue never seems to diminish.

48 Hours in Paris

Simon Calder takes a tour of the French Capital's First and Fourth arrondissements.

TRAVEL ESSENTIALS
Touch down

Eurostar trains (08705 186 186; eurostar.com) from London St Pancras, Ebbsfleet and Ashford arrive at the Gare du Nord. Flights from most UK airports arrive at Charles de Gaulle airport, 26km north. The city centre can be reached on line B of the suburban railway, the RER (ratp.info). A €9.25 ticket takes you to Gare du Nord and Châtelet.

Some flights arrive at Orly, 15km south. Take the Orlyval rail to Antony, where you change to the Métro network. A single is €10.70. The metro and RER suburban rail networks cover most of the city. Single tickets for journeys within the Paris boundaries cost €1.70, but a carnet of 10 tickets for €13.30 is more economical.

Get your bearings

This itinerary concentrates on the First and Fourth arrondissements, the most central districts on the Right Bank (north) of the River Seine. Within this ragged rectangle reside many of the city's treasures. The main tourist office is at 25 rue des Pyramides (00 33 8 92 68 30 00; parisinfo.com); open 10am-7.30pm daily.

Check in

Hotel-Résidence La Concorde, tucked in a courtyard at 5 rue Cambon (00 33 1 42 60 38 89; hotel-paris-concorde.com), has an optimistic three stars, but the staff are friendly and helpful and the location – a minute's walk from the Tuileries, and two minutes from Place de la Concorde – is excellent. The double-room rate is €155, including breakfast.

In a quiet street in the Marais, the 7e Art at 20 rue St-Paul (00 33 1 44 54 85 00; paris-hotel-7art.com) celebrates the silver screen.

Doubles with a cinematic ambience from €120, breakfast an extra €8 per person.

Or stray to the Left Bank, where the Hotel Quai Voltaire at 19 Quai Voltaire (00 33 1 42 61 50 91; quai voltaire.fr) has a double room rate of €135 (breakfast €11 per person). The rooms can feel cramped, and those on the lower floors are noisy, but it claims the best view of any hotel in Paris.

DAY ONE
Window shopping

Two grand department stores jostle for attention on Boulevard Haussmann: Galeries Lafayette (00 33 1 42 82 34 56; galerieslafayette.com) and Au Printemps (00 33 1 42 82 50 00; printemps.com). The displays are works of art. Open 9.30am-8pm daily except Sunday.

The Place du Marché St-Honoré is a stylish glass structure which is ringed by market stalls. To see how much haute couture sells for these days, check out a block or two along rue St- Honoré. But for a more intimate experience, the Galerie Vivienne is full of individual stores selling crafts and second-hand books, with Jean-Paul Gaultier just outside the western entrance and wine merchant Legrand Filles et Fils outside the eastern door.

Lunch on the run

Le Bougainville, at the eastern exit of Galerie Vivienne, at 5 rue de la Banque, is a lively, atmospheric café. Alternatively, visit the delicatessen Chez Marianne at 2 rue de l'Hospitalière (00 33 1 42 72 18 86; noon-midnight daily), where a pitta about the size of your head, filled with hot falafel and salad, costs €6.

Take a hike...

... around a corner of the Marais. From the exit of St-Paul Métro, head south down the narrow rue du Prévôt, flanked by bulging buildings. Turn left at the end along rue Charlemagne, then right along rue des Jardins St-Paul. Look for the pink sign saying "Village St-Paul" and wander through the courtyard full of artists' studios and workshops.

Emerge opposite the 7e-Art Hotel. Turn left up to rue St-Antoine, and go right. Look on the left for the Hotel de Sully at No 62, a former mansion now a cultural centre. Walk into the courtyard and keep going, possibly diverting into the excellent bookshop (open 10am to 7pm daily). Continue on the same trajectory to go through a door to emerge, possibly with some surprise, in the south-west corner of the Place des Vosges.

Picturesque embankment of the Seine

An aperitif

The Café Hugo at the north-east corner of the square is cosy, while the Delaville Café at 34 Boulevard Bonne Nouvelle (00 33 1 48 24 48 09; delavillecafe.com) is wilder. During happy hour (4-8pm), a glass of champagne is €6.

Dining with the locals

The southern end of Rue Montorgueil is packed with restaurants.

L'Esplanade Saint Eustache at 1 rue de Turbigo (00 33 1 50 08 53 03) is a cheerful bistro. Rump steak with frites and green salad is €14.50. L'Escargot at No 38 has been serving snails for two centuries. With a main course, expect to pay about €22, with dessert an extra €5. Le Petit Marcel at 65 rue Rambateau is tourist central, but good value: two courses start at €14.90, and include rabbit terrine with Calvados plus tartare classique.

DAY TWO
Sunday morning: go to church

The grand Parisian church that is probably visited less than any other is St-Germain l'Auxerrois (00 33 1 42 60 13 96; saintgermainauxerrois.cef.fr). Its magnificent rose window, the subject of a Claude Monet painting, faces the eastern end of the Louvre. Its foundations date from the 7th century. More recent additions include a handsome 15th-century wooden statue of Saint Germain (open Sundays 9am to 8pm, with masses at 9.45am and 11.30am; on other days, 8am to 7pm).

Out to brunch

At 5 rue de la Bastille, Bofinger (00 33 1 42 72 87 82; bofingerparis.com) serves hearty fare from Alsace daily from noon; try duck terrine to start, followed by a full-on Alsatian meat fest and see if you can walk out. The offering at Café Delaville (see An Aperitif) is lighter and cheaper (€23).

Cultural afternoon

The 400-year-old mansion in the south-east corner of the Place des Vosges, at No 6, is the Maison de Victor Hugo (00 33 1 42 72 10 16; bit.ly/HugoHere; 10am to 6pm daily except Mon and Tue; free) – where the writer lived in a second-floor apartment from 1832 to 1848. Besides writing Les Misérables here, he created some extravagant rooms. "I missed my vocation," he once said, "I was born to be an interior decorator." The Salon Chinois is the most striking, with an oriental fireplace inscribed "VH". Climb the elegant staircase all the way to the fourth floor to see some intriguing posters and photographs.

A walk in the park

Many tourists are drawn to the art collection within the Louvre, but for a fresh look consider the palace as a gateway to the Jardin de Tuileries. The existing garden was the location of the palace begun in

1561 by Catherine de Medici. The name arose because the location was the site of kilns making tiles.

Louis XIV ordered a new park to be created here in 1666. Interspersed with the trees are dozens of sculptures, including a Henry Moore and Rodin's Kiss close to the Musée de l'Orangerie (00 33 1 44 77 80 07; musee-orangerie.fr). This elegant museum was chosen by Monet to house his water-lilies paintings: eight curved canvases hang in two oval rooms. Open 9am to 6pm daily except Tuesdays, €7.50; free on the first Sunday of each month.

48 Hours in Reykjavik

With a busy cultural calendar, the Icelandic capital is an appealing prospect, says Nick Boulos.

TRAVEL ESSENTIALS
Touch down

International flights land at Keflavik airport, 48km west of Reykjavik. A taxi into the city will cost about ISK15,000 (£79.50). An airport bus shuttle offers a more cost-effective transfer. Flybus (00 354 580 5400; re.is/flybus) meets all arrivals with a return ticket to the BSI bus terminal costing ISK3,500 (£18.50). Journey time is about 50 minutes. For an extra ISK1,000 (£5) you'll be dropped off and picked up at your hotel.

Get your bearings

Ingolfur Arnarson came ashore from Norway in 872 and settled on a peninsula on the south-western corner of Iceland, naming it Reykjavik (meaning "Smoky Bay"). Located on the shores of Faxafloi Bay with Mount Esja (914m) and other peaks rising on the far side of the water, Reykjavik is easily explored on foot. The main sights, restaurants and shops are concentrated in the design district known as "101". Named after the postcode, it encompasses the streets around Laugavegur. The tourist information office is at Adalstraeti 2 (00 354 590 1550; visitreykjavik.is; open at 9am daily, to 6pm Monday-Friday, 4pm Saturday and 2pm Sunday). A 48-hour Reykjavik Welcome Card for unlimited public transport and entry to most museums costs ISK3,300 (£18).

Check in

Hotel Borg at 11 Posthusstraeti (00 354 551 1440; hotelborg.is) was the city's first luxury property when it opened in 1930. It still leads the way. Doubles start at ISK35,200 (£186), including breakfast.

Design lovers need look no further than Centerhotel Thingholt, well located at Thingholtsstraeti 3-5 (00 354 595 8530; centerhotels.com). Rooms are rugged yet hedonistic with bare concrete walls and leather floors. The decadent lobby bar features a wall made entirely from salmon scales. Doubles from ISK20,000 (£106), B&B.

It may, technically speaking, be a hostel but Kex at Skulagata 28 (00 354 560 6161; kexhostel.is) has more style than some five-star hotels. Movie set designer Halfdan Petiersen has transformed this former biscuit factory on the waterfront into a stunning property inspired by Fifties America. Dorm beds from ISK2,200 (£11) and doubles with private bathroom from ISK11,800 (£61), room only.

DAY ONE
Take a hike

Lake Tjornin and Reykjavik

Begin on the quiet shores of Lake Tjornin overlooking the modern City Hall, a building that divides opinion. Many locals think its industrial exterior is not in keeping with the area's heritage. This is the oldest part of the city, dating back to the 1760s. Walk along Tjarnargata before turning right on to Austurvollur, a leafy square and site for the world's oldest democracy: the understated Icelandic parliament building. Cross the square and travel north along Posthusstraeti before turning right on Tryggvagata, then left on to

Laekjargata. You'll soon emerge on the waterfront facing futuristic Harpa concert hall, set against a mountainous backdrop. Then walk west along Geirsgata.

Lunch on the run

Stop at the indoor Kolaportid flea market (00 354 562 5030; open 10am to 5pm weekends) to try Iceland's favourite snack: crisp-like pieces of dried fish. Or head for the collection of harbour wharf restaurants on Geirsgata, grab a stool and enjoy a steaming bowl of soup from locally caught lobster at Saegreifinn (00 354 553 1500; saegreifinn.is). Open 11.30am to 10pm daily.

Window shopping

Big-name brands are noticeably absent from Reykjavik's main shopping street, Skolavordustigur. Hours are short: typically 10am to 4pm on Saturdays (to 6pm Mon-Fri, closed Sundays). Fashion boutique Nostrum at No 1a (nostrum.is; open from 11am) sells wares only from Icelandic designers. Minja at No 12 (00 354 578 6090; minja.is) is a trendy interiors store.

Cultural afternoon

The National Museum at Sudurgata 41 (00 354 530 2200; nationalmuseum.is; 10am to 5pm daily, closed Mondays between mid-Sept and the end of April; ISK1,200/£6.50) should be your first port of call. Detailing 1,200 years of history, it traces Iceland's journey from settlement to modern day.

Later, investigate the country's thriving art scene. Erro, famed for his collages and mosaics with political undertones, has a permanent exhibition at the Reykjavik Art Museum (00 354 590 1200; artmuseum.is; open 10am to 5pm weekends, other days vary; ISK1,100/£6.90) – not to be confused with the Reykjavik Art Gallery at Skulagata 30 (00 354 578 2060; reykjavikart gallery.is; 1-5pm weekends, 10am-6pm weekdays; free) which has abstract and figurative pieces by contemporary painters.

An aperitif

Islenski Barinn at Posthusstraeti 9 (00 354 578 2020; islen-skibarinn.is) sells more than 30 beers from micro-breweries across Iceland. Pints from ISK700 (£3.80). Alternatively, the darkened first-floor bar Boston at Laugavegur 28b (00 354 517 7816), with gold-leaf wallpaper and mirrored pillars, is a nice spot to sip brennivin – the potent national drink made from fermented potatoes and flavoured with cumin.

Dining with the locals

Tucked away in a residential street is Prir Frakkar at Baldursgata 14 (00 354 552 3939; 3frakkar.com). The crammed tables are testa-ment to the tasty food here. Dishes include wild guillemot breast with game sauce for ISK4,390 (£27).

Less adventurous diners who are still keen to try local produce should opt for Einar Ben at Veltusund 1 (00 354 511 5090; einarben.is). Go for the lamb loin with potato cakes for ISK5,100 (£27).

DAY TWO
Sunday morning: go to church

Dominating the city skyline is the striking Hallgrimskirkja church at the top of Skolavorouholt (00 354 510 1000; hallgrimskirkja.is), designed to resemble the basalt formations found across the country. Take a trip to the top of its 73m concrete bell tower (9am to 5pm daily; ISK700/£3.75) for views over the city's col-ourful rooftops.

The city's Domkirkjan cathedral (00 354 520 9700; domkirkjan.is), next door to the Parliament building, is closed at weekends except for Sunday service at 11am. Don't let the fact that it's conducted in Icelandic put you off; pop along for a glimpse of its impressive altar painted by G T Wegener in 1847.

Out to brunch

The trendy Laundromat Café at Austurstraeti 9 (00 354 587 7555; thelaundromatcafe.com), a Danish import, offers a dedicated brunch menu for saints and sinners, 10am to 4pm at weekends.

Choose between the "clean" (including scrambled eggs, homemade hummus and fruit) or the "dirty" (spicy sausage, bacon and a rich local cheese) for ISK1,990 (£10). There are also fresh fruit juices, grilled sandwiches and the opportunity to wash your smalls in the laundrette downstairs.

A walk in the park

Reykjavik's best walking is Oskjuhlid, a forested hill just outside the city centre with the Pearl, a local landmark of six vast aluminium tanks and a glass dome, sitting at the crown. Gentle trails weave through pine woodland with views over the city and mountains from the top. Take a stroll down to Nautholsvik, a geothermal beach with sand imported from the western fjords.

Take a ride ...

... into the wild. Head out to sea to spot puffins (May-Aug) and humpback and orca whales on a wildlife cruise with Elding (00 354 555 3565; elding.is). Three-hour trips leave daily at 1pm from the harbour and cost ISK8,500 (£45).

Icing on the cake

At the Blue Lagoon, close to the airport (00 354 420 8800; bluelagoon.com; ISK5000/£26.50), plumes of steam rise from the milky waters surrounded by hills of jagged and blackened lava. But for a more local experience visit one of Reykjavik's 18 tourist-free city baths, all shown at swimminginiceland.com. Bjork's favourite is reputed to be Vesturbaejarlaug (00 354 411 5150; 9am to 5pm Saturday, 11am to 7pm Sunday, weekdays vary) on Hofsvallagata, with a large outdoor pool and four bubbling hot tubs at 35-39C.

48 Hours in Riga

Visit the Latvian capital to experience its rich medieval and Art Nouveau architecture. By William Cook.

TRAVEL ESSENTIALS
Touch down

Riga's airport (00 371 293 11187; riga-airport.com) is 8km west of the city centre. Bus 22 takes 30 minutes to reach the city centre.

Buses depart from 5am (6am at weekends) until 11.30pm. A single ticket costs €0.70 from the tourist information bureau in the arrivals hall, or €1 from the driver (00 371 8000 1919; rigassatiksme.lv).

Alight at 11 Novembra Krastmala for the old town. A taxi costs about €13 and takes 15 to 20 minutes.

Get your bearings

Riga is the biggest city in the Baltic states – and the joint European Capital of Culture for 2014 (along with Umea in Sweden). Most of its main landmarks are within walking distance of the compact city centre. The majority of the historic sites are situated in the beautifully preserved old town – a jumble of medieval and Renaissance buildings on the east bank of the Daugava river.

Further east, beyond the pretty City Park lies one of Europe's largest concentrations of unspoilt Art Nouveau architecture.

Riga's tourist office is at Ratslaukums 6 (00 371 6703 7900; liveriga.com; 10am-6pm daily) on the main square. The flamboyant building in which it's housed, a 14th-century guildhall, is an attraction in its own right.

Check in

Built in 1877 as the head office of the Bank of Latvia, the Grand Palace Hotel at Pils 12 (00 371 6704 4000; grandpalaceriga.com) enjoys a prime location in the heart of the old town. Doubles start at €179, including breakfast.

In the shadow of the cathedral, Gutenbergs at Doma Laukums 1 (00 371 6781 4090; gutenbergs.eu) is a homely four-star converted from a printworks, with an old-fashioned interior that's quiet and cosy. Doubles start at €69, including breakfast.

The three-star Hotel Hanza is an excellent budget option. It is in a cobbled square beside a wooden church at Elijas 7 (00 371 6779 6040; hanzahotel.lv). Doubles from just €40, including breakfast. There's even a small spa. It's a short walk from the main train station and the bustling Central Market, which is housed in three huge Zeppelin hangars.

DAY ONE
Take a ride

Riga City Tour buses (00 371 2665 5405; citytour.lv) depart from Latviesu Strelnieku Laukums between 10am and 3pm daily. Tickets cost €15 and are valid for 48 hours. You can hop off and on at a dozen stops along the way. The route takes in the old town, new Riga (the Art Nouveau district) and wooden Riga (the traditional timber houses on the west bank of the Daugava). The tour takes between 60 and 90 minutes, depending on traffic.

Take a view

Take the lift up the spire of St Peter's Church at Skarnu 19, a short walk from the Latviesu Strelnieku Laukums, where the tour buses terminate (00 371 6718 1943; peterbaznica.riga.lv). Tickets cost €7 and also include admission to the church, which doubles as an art gallery. The ticket office is open 10am-5.30pm Tuesday to Saturday and from noon to 6pm on Sunday. The view from the top is breathtaking, but this UNESCO-listed Lutheran church – which was originally founded in 1209 by the Germanic crusaders who established Riga – is also well worth a visit.

Old Town from Saint Peter's

Lunch on the run

Located around the corner from St Peter's, Province at Kalku 2 (00 371 6722 2566; provincija.lv) is the perfect pit stop. The décor is quaint and folksy, the food is nourishing and hearty. A big bowl of cabbage soup with pork and potatoes, followed by bread pudding with cream, figs and nuts, washed down with half a litre of cold, strong lager, costs €13.10.

Take a hike

Brivibas iela ("Freedom Street") is like a timeline of the last century. A walk along this busy boulevard constitutes a crash course in Latvian history. Start at Latviesu Strelnieku Laukums, beneath the statue of the Latvian riflemen who fought for Lenin. Head east along Kalku iela, past rows of handsome houses built by German merchants, to the graceful Freedom Monument erected during Latvia's first era of independence, between the wars.

Further along is Riga's Russian Orthodox Cathedral, a planetarium during the Soviet occupation, now a place of worship once again. End outside the former KGB HQ on the junction of Stabu iela and Brivibas iela. A plaque remembers the countless Latvians who were imprisoned, tortured and killed there.

Window shopping

Latvia's most iconic export is Latvijas balzams, a potent liqueur in a black bottle that's distilled to an eye-watering 45-per-cent proof. Catherine the Great fell ill when she came here, and was cured by a stiff shot of it – well, that's the story. You can buy it in 50 shops around Riga – visit lb.lv or call 00 371 6708 12 13 for details.

Contents include raspberries, bilberries, ginger, nutmeg, linden blossom and valerian root. The acquired taste resembles a cross between Jagermeister and cough mixture.

For a less boozy souvenir, visit Pienene at Kungu 7/9 (00 371 6721 0400; studijapienene.lv; 10am-8pm daily) which sells products made by local artisans, including clothes, cosmetics and children's toys. The shop contains a stylish café, selling handmade truffles.

An aperitif

Alberta Street is the hub of Riga's Art Nouveau district and the best place to drink in the view is from the top floor of the high-rise Albert Hotel at Dzirnavu 23 (00 371 6733 1717; alberthotel.lv).

The penthouse lounge is a laid-back bar, with DJs from 8pm and draught beers from €3.

Dining with the locals

A block away from the Albert Hotel is Restorans Alberta 1221 at Antonijas 13 (00 371 6733 6500; alberta1221.lv). The décor is modern, the menu is European with a contemporary twist: goulash with apricots, sturgeon and salmon borsch. Three courses cost around €22, without wine.

DAY TWO
Sunday morning: go to church

Riga's magnificent brick cathedral on Doma Laukums (00 371 6722 7573; doms.lv; 10am-5pm daily; €4.30, except for worship) is the biggest medieval building in Latvia. It was founded in 1211 by the Teutonic Knights who established this Hanseatic port in the 13th century. There are services in German at 10am (except for the first Sunday of the month) and in Latvian at noon on Sundays, and organ recitals on Wednesdays and Saturdays at noon, admission €7.

Out to brunch

The island of Kipsala, with its old wooden houses, is the ideal destination for a Sunday morning stroll, and Ostas Skati at Matrozu 15 (00 371 6750 8658; ostasskati.lv) is a sublime setting for Sunday brunch. This sleek waterfront restaurant has lovely views of the old town, across the River Daugava. The buffet costs €11.25, including coffee. It's always popular, so best to book ahead.

A walk in the park

The Freedom Monument is the best starting point for a wander around Riga's City Park. Follow the canal north to the Congress Centre or south to the Opera House. In summer, you can take a boat trip along the canal and out into the Daugava river (00 371 2591 1523; kmk.lv).

Cultural afternoon

Built in 1923, in ornate Rococo style, the Splendid Palace at Elizabetes 61 (00 371 6718 1143; splendidpalace.lv) was the first cinema in the Baltic states to show talkies. Ninety years later it's still a working cinema, showing a wide range of European films and live transmissions from foreign opera houses. Riga Story, a 30- minute documentary screened daily in English at 10am, noon and 2pm, is a useful introduction to the history of this extraordinary city. Admission is €7.10.

Icing on the cake

Designed by a German from St Petersburg in the style of a Venetian palazzo, Riga Bourse epitomises the Latvian capital's eclectic heritage. The old stock exchange at Doma laukums 6 has been lovingly restored, and is now a palatial art museum (00 371 6722 3434; lnmm.lv; 10am-6pm daily except Monday, until 8pm on Friday). The permanent collection features a respectable selection of Dutch and Flemish Masters, and a spectacular haul of Meissen porcelain.

48 Hours in Rome

The Italian capital is packed with tourist must-sees, says Nick Boulos.

TRAVEL ESSENTIALS
Touch down

Rome's main airport is Fiumicino, 26km south-east of the centre. The Leonardo Express train (trenitalia.com) departs every half hour from 6.38am to 11.38pm and takes 31 minutes to reach the central station, Roma Termini. A one-way fare is €14. For €8, you can catch the FR1 train connecting with the city's Metro system at Ostiense and Tiburtina stations. A taxi to the city centre will cost about €50.

Ciampino airport, 15km south of the centre, is served by Ryanair. Trains make the 15-minute journey from Ciampino Citta station – a few minutes away and connected by shuttle buses (€1) – to Termini four times an hour. A one-way ticket costs €1.30; a taxi will set you back €30.

Get your bearings

Founded in 753BC and famously built upon seven hills, Rome was the beating heart of the Roman Empire. The city became Italy's capital in 1871. It is bisected north-south by the Tiber; you'll find the remains of ancient Rome and most famous sights to the east. To the north-west is the walled sovereign state of Vatican City. A third of the size of London's Hyde Park, it was granted independence by Mussolini in 1929.

The handiest tourist office is at Via Giovanni Giolitti 34 near Termini station. There are several others across the city (turismoroma.it; open 9.30am-7pm daily). A three-day Roma Pass (romapass.it; €34) offers reduced entry to some attractions, plus free public transport.

Check in

Sitting atop Monte Mario, the tallest of the city's hills, the Rome Cavalieri (00 39 06 35091; romecavalieri.com) at Via Alberto Cadlolo 101 is a sumptuous hotel with rare Flemish tapestries, antique Louis XV furniture and art by Giambattista Tiepolo and Andy Warhol. Doubles start at €300, including breakfast.

Albergo del Sole opened in 1467 on Piazza della Rotonda (00 39 06 678 0441; hotelsolealpantheon.com). Past guests include princes, poets and politicians. Doubles from around €150, B&B.

Hearth Hotel (00 39 06 39 03 83 83; hearthhotel.com) is centrally situated in front of the entrance to the Vatican museums. The rooms are clean and spacious and you can breakfast on the roof terrace; doubles from €120, B&B

DAY ONE
Cultural morning

Rise early to beat the crowds at the Vatican Museums (00 39 06 698 84676; mv.vatican.va; €16). The highlight is the Sistine Chapel with its intricate frescos painted by a reluctant Michelangelo, who considered himself a sculptor. It opens 9am-6pm Mon to Sat and on the last Sunday of every month when entrance is free. Don't leave without marvelling at the opulence of St Peter's Basilica.

Alternatively, head to the Roman Forum (00 39 06 399 67 700; pierreci.it; €15.50). The ruins were once official buildings and temples, some built by Julius Caesar. Admission also includes fast- track entry to the Colosseum. The crumbling amphitheatre was first used for gladiatorial battles in AD80, staged in front of 50,000 jeering spectators. Open 8.30am-7pm daily (4pm in winter).

Basilica of St Peter, Vatican City

Roman Colosseum

Take a hike

Start at Bernini's Fountain of the Four Rivers in the middle of Piazza Navona. Head east and cross Palazzo Madama, until you reach the Corinthian columns of the Pantheon. This 2nd-century temple, built by Emperor Hadrian, features an oculus in the roof, casting a column of sunlight (and sometimes rain) on to the marble floor (9am-7.30pm Mon to Sat, to 5.30pm Sun; free).

Walk along Via del Seminario; turn left on Via del Corso and take the second right on to Via delle Muratte to reach the Trevi Fountain. Throw a coin in (legend has it that those who do will one day return), before walking along Via Poli.Cross Via del Tritone and pause for an espresso at Angelina (00 39 06 679 7274; ristoranteangelina.com) at Via Poli 27, a café with concrete floors and ceilings hung with empty birdcages.

Turn right on Via del Bufalo and take the first left. Stay on Via di Propaganda until you emerge at Piazza Mignanelli and the Spanish Steps: Francesco de Sanctis's 138-step staircase leading to the Trinita dei Monti church.

Lunch on the run

Hostaria da Pietro (00 39 06 320 8816; hostariadapietro.com) is a small restaurant tucked away down the narrow Via Gesu e Maria 18. The pasta is heavenly, the desserts homemade (try the crème caramel) and the waiters chatty. Mains from €14.

Window shopping

Via del Babuino is lined with eclectic stores: contemporary fashion at Pinko (No 92) and Iceberg (No 87); fine art from Carlucci (No 192); and, if your budget stretches to it, antiques from the 1700s at W Apolloni (No 133).

An aperitif

Caffe della Pace (00 39 06 686 1216; caffedellapace.it) is a pleasant spot for a pre-dinner tipple. The Art Deco-inspired interior is cosy; however, the outdoor tables, overlooking a small square, are highly sought after.

Dining with the locals

Il Corallo at Via del Corallo 10 (00 39 06 683 07703; bit.ly/Il-Corallo) is a small pizzeria popular with locals and Hollywood stars. There are 23 tempting options.

Taverna Trilussa at Via del Politeama 23/25 (00 39 06 581 8918; tavernatrilussa.it), is a charming restaurant specialising in hearty pasta dishes. Bucatini all'amatriciana is a local favourite.

DAY TWO
Sunday morning: go to church

You're spoilt for choice, with nearly 1,000 churches to select from. Santa Maria Maggiore at Piazza di Santa Maria Maggiore 42 (00 39 06 483195) may not be one of the best known, but it's undoubtedly special. Under its vast Baroque dome is a staircase designed by Bernini and mosaics from the 5th century. Visitors are welcome to attend Sunday mass, which is held on the hour between 7am-noon (except 11am). Open 7am-7pm daily.

Out to brunch

Beyond the wholemeal cakes, trays of rustici (savoury pastries stuffed with everything from ricotta to salmon) and bread shaped like the Colosseum, the bakery and deli Panella at Via Merulana 54 (00 39 06 487 2435; panella-artedelpane.it) puts on an all-you-can- eat brunch (€15) every Sunday, 10am-2pm.

Take a view

Giuseppe Sacconi's white marble masterpiece Il Vittoriano (00 39 06 699 1718), on Piazza Venezia, was built as a monument to Italy's first king. Take the lift (€7) to the viewing platform from where a sea of terracotta rooftops punctuated by bulbous domes and long boulevards spread out below you (9.30am-10.30pm Fri-Sun, to 6.30pm other days).

A walk in the park

The landscaped grounds of Villa Borghese started out as vineyards and sprawling family estates until 1605 when the nephew of Pope Paul V had better ideas. Today, it's Rome's largest and loveliest park with quiet duck ponds, Ionic temples and several museums – most notably the Borghese Gallery (00 39 06 841 3979; galleriaborghese.it; 8.30am-7.30pm daily except Mon; €11) with works by Raphael and Caravaggio. Tickets must be pre-booked.

Take a ride

How better to see the sights than on a vintage Vespa? Those not brave enough to take on Rome's fast and frenzied roads themselves can leave the hard work to a professional. A four-hour tour costs €150 with Bici Baci (00 39 06 945 39240; bicibaci.com).

Icing on the cake

Gelato king Stefano Marcotulli has become something of a modern day Willy Wonka, thanks to the experimental flavours in his aptly named ice-cream parlour Gelateria del Teatro (00 39 06 454 74880) at Via di San Simone 70. He uses only the finest ingredients – lemons from Amalfi and pistachios from Sicily – and the more unique offerings include white chocolate and basil, or raspberry with garden sage. Scoops start from €2.50.

Cultural afternoon

The ship's remains are housed in the Vasa Museum, which reopened this year after refurbishment (00 46 8 519 548 00; www.vasamuseet.se; 10am-5pm daily, Wednesday to 8pm, SEK130/£13). It tells of how, on 10 August 1628, the Vasa set sail but sank after 15 minutes. For the next 333 years she lay in the harbour's mud until she was resurrected and rehoused.

Vasa ship in the Vasa Museum

A walk in the park

Close by is the main entrance to Skansen, a Scandinavian theme park aimed at rescuing Sweden's heritage from the march of progress (00 46 8 442 8000; skansen.se; open daily at 10am; closing times vary seasonally; SEK110 /£11). Like Alfred Nobel, Artur Hazelius was wealthy, enlightened and altruistic. In 1891, as Sweden raced towards an industrial future, he decided to preserve the traditional way of life and dozens of buildings from across the country have been relocated here. Costumed guides reveal how simple, and tough, Nordic life was.

Icing on the cake

Emerge from the main gate of Skansen and cross the road to ABBA The Museum at Djurgardsvagen 68 (00 46 8 12 13 28 60; ab-bathemuseum.com; 10am to 8pm daily; SEK195/£19.50). There was something in the air that night in Brighton in 1974, when the four-somewon the Eurovision Song Contest. Abba went on to dominate the charts for a decade. The museum reveals how Agnetha, Bjorn, Benny and Frida formed and later fell apart. "Walk in and dance out," says the publicity. "It feels like we've come home," says Bjorn.

end of Russian rule. Tours cost €16pp and run daily (even in winter), starting at 11am, from outside the offices of operator, City Bike at Uus 33 in the Old Town (00 372 51 11819; citybike.ee).

A walk in the park

The city's main park, a 20-minute walk to the west of the Old Town (00 372 601 5783; kadriorupark.ee), is named after the district it is found in: Kadriorg. This 300-year-old open space hosts two fine art galleries. Kadriorg Palace is where you'll find Russian and western European art and a magnificent Baroque main hall (00 372 606 6400; kadriorumuuseum.ee; 10am-5pm Thursday-Sunday, 10am-8pm Wednesday, closed Monday and Tuesday; €4.80). The imposing Kumu is home to the national art collection (00 372 602 6000; kumu.ee; 11am-6pm Thursday-Sunday, 11am-8pm Wednesday, closed Monday and Tuesday; €5.50).

Kadriorg Palace

Out to brunch

A gig venue during the evening, Von Krahli Baar at 10 Rataskaevu 10123 (00 372 626 9096; vonkrahl.ee) has good Estonian and international cuisine at bargain prices in the daytime. Try the smoked cheese and tomato soup (€2.50), or pasta with shrimp and salmon (€4).

Cultural afternoon

Destroyed by Second World War bombing, St Nicholas' Church at Niguliste 3 (00 372 53431052; nigulistemuuseum.ee; open Wednesday-Sunday 10am-5pm, €3.50) now houses religious art and silver items, including a 16th-century silver parrot and the 7.5m-long, 15th-century Danse Macabre, one of the finest examples of this medieval genre.

Icing on the cake

The Seaplane Harbour, housed in concrete former seaplane hangars by the Kalamaja shore, is a modern, interactive maritime and military history museum (00 372 6 200 550; lennusadam.eu; Tuesday-Sunday 10am-7pm, €10).

traditional Maltese harbour boat, provided by A&S Water Taxis (00 356 2180 6921; maltesewatertaxis.com; €10 for 30 minutes).

Out to brunch

Sundays can be quiet, with many shops and restaurants closed, but the handsome old Caffe Cordina at 244 Republic Street (00 356 2123 4385; www.caffecordina.com) opens 8.30am to 7pm. Sit outside under Queen Victoria's gaze with pastizzi – the most popular local snack, a mini pasty of cheese or peas. It is also a great place to buy such specialist Maltese foods as local capers, honey and antipasti (packed for travel).

Cultural afternoon

Jump on a bus out of town to the remarkable Mnajdra and Hagar Qim temples (00 356 214 231; heritagemalta.org), which are the best preserved of Malta's Neolithic stone temples. These remains, built between 3600 and 2500BC, are older than the Great Pyramids and Stonehenge. The excellent on-site exhibition will reveal all, before you wander around the temples with their monumental entrance-ways, tightly packed stone walls, semi-circular rooms and carved altars. Open daily; admission €9.

Icing on the cake

At the convivial little Legligin, a restaurant and wine bar at 117 Santa Lucia Street (00 356 2122 1699), Chris cooks all the food, chooses all the wine, and holds court. His Maltese mezze (€20) is a feast of nine mini (and not-so-mini) traditional dishes – including rabbit stew. Round the evening off with his homemade limoncello liqueur.

48 Hours in Vienna

This handsome city offers luxury, shopping and great green spaces, says Anthony Lambert.

TRAVEL ESSENTIALS
Touch down

The airport is on S-Bahn line S7 which delivers you to Landstrasse/Wien Mitte for €3.60. The 16-minute City Airport Train to the same station costs €9 and operates at half-hourly intervals between 6.05am and 11.35pm. The airport is 10 miles south east of the city; taxis cost around €30.

Get your bearings

The former Habsburg capital of the Austro-Hungarian Empire retains the architectural grandeur of its powerful rulers. Their legacy forms most of Vienna's tourist attractions, from palaces to museums, complemented by an overlay of outstanding Secessionist buildings and a still-dynamic cultural scene.

The historic Inner City (Innere Stadt) is held within the Ringstrasse, which was built on the line of the old city fortifications, demolished in the mid-19th century. To the north-west lie wine villages, while to the east of the Inner City, the Danube Canal meanders through the urban fabric.

The efficient underground (U-Bahn), S-Bahn, tram and bus network is the best way to get around, though there is also a London-style bike-hire scheme. The 72-hour Vienna Card costs €19, and includes use of city transport as well as attraction discounts. It is available at the Tourist Information Office behind the State Opera House at Albertinaplatz. Open daily 9am-7pm (00 43 1 24 555; vienna.info).

Check in

Among Vienna's many five-star hotels, Hotel Palais Coburg at Coburgbastei 4 (00 43 1 51818 0; coburg.at) is perhaps the most stunning. It was built in the 1840s as the palace of the House of Coburg-Gotha and its conversion to an all-suite hotel skilfully blends modern with old. Doubles from €670, B&B.

Part of a small and quirky chain, the 25 Hours Hotel, Lerchenfelderstrasse 1-3 (00 43 152 1510; 25hours-hotels.com) takes as its theme the circus and incorporates memorabilia from the city's three permanent circus buildings. Doubles from €130, room only. Meanwhile, Pension Residenz is a traditionally furnished hotel at Ebendorferstrasse 10 (00 43 1 406 47 86 0; residenz.cc).

Doubles from €90, B&B.

DAY ONE
Take a hike

Starting at the Tourist Information Office on Albertinaplatz, walk along Augustinerstrasse past the Albertina. With 21 state rooms and the world's largest collection of drawings and graphics (00 43 1 534 83 0; albertina.at; open daily 10am-6pm; €11), it is one end of the vast complex of Habsburg buildings known as the Hofburg, which contains enough museums and sights, including the Spanish Riding School, to absorb days (00 43 1 533 7570; hofburg-wien.at; €10.50).

Take Kohlmarkt to reach Petersplatz and the baroque Peterskirche (peterskirche.at), consecrated in 1733 and built on the site of Vienna's first church, erected as part of the Roman camp of Vindobona. Unusually, the painted decoration of the oval cupola has been married with plasterwork to enhance the illusion of three dimensions.

Join the pedestrianised streets around the cathedral, Stephansdom, which is regarded as the finest gothic building in Austria and still has Turkish cannonballs embedded in it, as well as iconic diamond- patterned roof tiles (00 43 1 515 523 540; stephanskirche.at).

Continue along Rotenturmstrasse to reach Schwedenplatz and a good place for coffee or a drink: Motto am Flus (00 43 1 25 25512; motto.at/mottoamfluss) is in a stylish modern structure on stilts overlooking the Danube Canal.

Window shopping

There is a concentration of small antique and curio shops in the streets between Peterskirche and the cathedral and a delightful period shop selling superb chocolates: Leschanz is at Freisingergasse 1 (00 43 1 533 3219; schokoladekoenig.at).

Lunch on the run

Close to Stephansplatz at Weihburggasse 17 is Gasthaus Poschl (00 43 1 513 5288), where beneath a vaulted ceiling you can enjoy a lunch of pumpkin soup (€3.90), schnitzel with potato salad (€17.50) and apple and poppy seed strudel with vanilla sauce (€5.50).

Cultural afternoon

Prince Eugene of Savoy acquired such wealth from his victories over the Turks that he created the opulent palace and garden of the Belvedere in the early 18th century "without undue burdening of his purse". The Upper Belvedere now houses an art collection that spans over four centuries and has the world's largest collection of paintings by Gustav Klimt, including The Kiss. The building and grounds alone are worth a visit (00 43 1 79 557 0; belvedere.at; daily 10am-6pm; €14 combined entry).

An aperitif

The Sofitel Stephansdom, designed by Jean Nouvel at Praterstrasse 1 (00 43 1 906 160; sofitel.com) boasts the 18th-floor Le Loft bar and restaurant with spectacular westerly views over the city. Order a glass of wine for €4.90 and sip beneath a ceiling decorated with a colourful autumn leaf scene by the Swiss artist Pipilotti Rist.

Dining with the locals

Near the Museums Quarter at Sigmundsgasse 1/1 is Kulinarium 7, a wine merchant with a restaurant attached (00 43 1 522 33 77; kulinarium7.at). Dishes such as avocado and tomato tart with olive foam (€9), pan-fried duck breast with pak choy and mushroom schupf noodles (€23) and Baileys parfait with coffee sauce (€8) can be enjoyed either at the counter or conventional tables.

DAY TWO
Sunday morning: go to church

The Karlskirche is Vienna's most celebrated baroque building, designed by Fischer von Erlach after winning a competition set up by Charles VI. The church is dedicated to the carer of plague victims, St Charles Borromeo of Milan, following the death of 8,000 people here in 1713. Start your visit by exploring its surroundings, including a tranquil expanse of water and central sculpture by Henry Moore. You can enter the church at noon, to gaze upwards at the huge oval copper dome flanked by tall columns carrying the story of St Charles carved in a spiral frieze (00 43 1 504 61 87; www.karlskirche.at; Sun noon-5.45pm; €6).

Saint Charles church

Take a view...

...from the top of the south tower of the Stephansdom. You reach a height of over 60 metres up a narrow spiral staircase, having paid €3.50 at the entrance. There is only one resting place going up or down the 343 steps – the bench used by Count Ernst Rudiger von Starhemberg as a look-out when commanding the forces defending the city against the Turks in 1683. The tower is open from 9am-5.30pm. The north tower viewing platform is considerably lower but has a lift.

Out to brunch

The music of Johann Strauss accompanies an Art Brunch under wood panelled ceilings and 19th-century frescos by Carl Rahl at Palais Todesco at Karntnerstrasse 51 (00 43 1 743 4422 7861; gerstner.at). Reservations for the €43 brunch are recommended.

Take a ride

A ride around the Ringstrasse on tram D takes you around the circle of civic buildings and bourgeois villas created after the order of 1857 to demolish the city's fortifications. It runs daily from 10am-6pm and costs €7. The first trip of the day starts at Opera; the end station is Schwedenplatz, where the tram arrives every 15 and 45 minutes past the hour; you can get on and off at any tram stop en route.

A walk in the park

Vienna has the highest ratio of green space in any European city. Families head for the vast Prater, with its playgrounds, miniature railway and observation wheel, reached from Messe-Prater station. Meanwhile, the Augarten, close to Taborstrasse, has within its 52 hectares the oldest baroque garden in Vienna.

The icing on the cake

Vienna is synonymous with the Secessionists, and their emblematic building at Friedrichstrasse 12 remains one of the city's most extraordinary structures, with its cupola of golden laurel leaves and art nouveau façade.

Called simply the Secession Building, it was designed by Joseph Maria Olbricht as an exhibition hall. The Beethoven Frieze painted by Klimt in 1902 in homage to the composer can still be admired. It can be reached from Karlsplatz station and is open daily except Monday, 10am-6pm, admission €8.50 (00 43 1 5875 307; secession.at) runs daily from 10am-6pm and costs €7. The first trip of the day starts at Opera; the end station is Schwedenplatz, where the tram arrives every 15 and 45 minutes past the hour; you can get on and off at any tram stop en route.

48 Hours in Warsaw

Head to the Polish capital to experience designer shops and striking modern architecture, says Mary Lussiana.

TRAVEL ESSENTIALS
Touch down

Warsaw's main airport, Frederic Chopin, is 10km south of the centre. Bus 175 takes around 45 minutes to reach Central Railway station, leaving every 15 minutes between 5am and 11pm. A night bus, N32, also runs. Tickets (4.40 zloty, written 4.40 PLN/90p) are available from kiosks with the RUCH logo; validate your ticket in the machine as you enter. Taxis take around 20 minutes and cost 35 to 40 PLN (£7-8); choose registered taxis such as Super Taxi, Sawa Taxi or Ele. Trains also run into the city centre every 15 minutes, taking around 20 minutes to Central station (bit.ly/WarsawTrains, singles 4.40PLN (90p).

Some flights serve Modlin, 35km north-west. The Modlin Bus (00 48 801 801 081; see modlinbus.com for timetables) takes anything from an hour to an hour-and-a-half to reach the Palace of Culture and Science; one-way fares start at 9 PLN (£1.80).

Get your bearings

The Polish capital is looking better than ever. The flourishing economy has helped create designer shops, new restaurants, a plethora of recent museum openings and striking modern architecture – Daniel Libeskind's eye-catching Zlota 44 is the city's tallest residential building. The Soviets' present to the Poles, the hideous and dominating Palace of Culture and Science is the inevitable landmark in Central Warsaw, standing near Central station and between several main arteries. It houses the Tourist Office (00 48 22 194 31; warsawtour.pl; 8am to 6pm daily, until 8pm from April to September).

Warsaw is easy to navigate, with an excellent system of trams, metro and buses. Most of the historic sites lie along the Royal Route, which leads from the Royal Castle in the old Town – the whole of which was beautifully rebuilt in the decades after its destruction in the Second World War – south to Wilanow Palace, and runs parallel, but on higher ground, to the Vistula river. Commercial and business districts spread out west of the Royal Route with the leafy residential district of Zoliborz marking Warsaw's north.

Warsaw's Old Town and Royal Castle

Check in

The deluxe Hotel Bristol, a recent addition to Starwood's Luxury Collection, brims with history, with Art Deco interiors and the best location in town on the Royal Route at 42/44 Krakowskie Przedmiescie (00 48 22 55 11 00; luxurycollection.com/bristolwarsaw). Doubles start at 439 PLN (£89) room only.

Newly renovated and nicely central, the comfortable four-star Hotel Mercure Warszawa Grand offers value at 28 Krucza Street (00 48 22 583 2100; mercure.com). Doubles start at 217 PLN (£43) room only.

With a reputation as Warsaw's best budget option, the Hotel Campanile has free Wi-Fi, a good buffet breakfast and a relatively central location at 2 Towarowa (00 48 22 582 7200; campanile.com). Doubles from 153 PLN (£30) room only.

DAY ONE
Take a view

Warsaw wags claim the city's best view is from the top of the 230-metre high Palace of Culture and Science because you can't see it. It does, however, give you an overview of the city. Open 9am to 6pm; tickets 20 PLN/£4 (00 48 22 656 76 00).

Take a hike

Start in the old town market square and walk along the cobbled streets, dipping in and out of the amber shops until you reach the Royal Castle. From here, head down the main thoroughfare of Krakowskie Przedmiescie, past the Neoclassical Presidential Palace and swerving off to the right for the Tomb of the Unknown Soldier where an eternal flame burns, soldiers stand guard and dignitaries come to lay wreaths.

As you continue along Krakowskie Przedmiescie, stop at the Holy Cross Church to see where Frédéric Chopin's heart is buried. Continue on to the beautiful Plac Trzech Krzyzy with its neoclassical Saint Aleksander's Church. Go beyond to Aleje Ujazdowskie, where the wide avenue is lined on one side by embassies and on the other by a park. Finish at Belvedere Palace, whose image is etched on vodka bottles and where President Komorowski resides.

Lunch on the run

Grab some potato pancakes or pierogi (dumplings with a variety of stuffings). Most Polish restaurants will have a variation on the theme but the new Dawne Smaki at 49 Nowy Swiat (00 48 22 465 83 20; dawnesmaki.pl) specialises in these delicious traditional dishes – quick, filling and cheap, from 19 PLN (£3.80).

Window shopping

Mokotowksa Street jostles with Polish designers' ateliers, such as Ania Kuczynska (00 48 22 622 0276; aniakuczynska.com) at No 61, jewellery opposite at Lilou (No 63; 00 48 22 403 19 19; lilou.pl) and fashion and homeware at Maciej Zien (00 48 519 000 049; zien.pl) at No 57. For homespun goods, try Cepelia handicraft store (00 48 22 621 26 18; cepelia.pl) at Plac Konstytucji 5, where traditional cribs mix with painted wooden birds, hand-embroidered linen and bold woven rugs.

An aperitif

The Bristol Wine Bar (00 48 22 55 11 00; luxurycollection.com/bristolwarsaw) at the Hotel Bristol is a must. Pavement tables allow you to watch the world go by in elegant surroundings; wine by the glass starts at 18 PLN (£3.50). For a more informal feel head to Beirut Hummus and Music Bar at Poznanska 12. It's a humming, happening place where you can try a few Polish beers or vodkas along with the speciality olive oil-soaked hummus.

Dining with the locals

For a more traditional setting, try U Kucharzy at Ujazdowskie 8 (00 48 22 826 79 36; gessler.pl) for the sour rye soup, chanterelle mushrooms in cream, or roast duck stuffed with apple; main dishes around 50 PLN (£10). A favourite with the "in crowd" is Zushi Sushi at Zurawia 6/12 (00 48 22 420 33 73 74) which has an impressive range of sashimi, sushi, nigiri, maki (items from 20 PLN /£4) and sake.

DAY TWO
Sunday morning: go to church

Churches abound in this Catholic country and there are many masses throughout the morning. The Church of the Nuns of the Visitation at Krakowskie Przedmiescie 34 is a little Baroque jewel where young Chopin often came to play the organ. There are six masses from 7.30am to 5pm, otherwise opening hours on Sunday are from 1pm to 4.30pm, weekdays from 9.30am, Saturday 9am to 2pm (00 48 22 826 65 85; wizytki.waw.pl).

Out to brunch

Try the Brasserie Warszawska on a quiet side street, 24 Górnoslaska Street, near the Parliament (00 48 22 628 94 23; brasseriewarszaw ska.pl). It has a Sunday menu of fresh oysters, beef tartare and wild Baltic salmon; dishes from 25 PLN (£5).

A walk in the park

Adjacent is the leafy Ujazdowskie Park, which was first laid out in 1896, the wide avenues lead to a lake, waterfall and bridges, delivering serenity in the heart of the city.

Cultural afternoon

You can't come to Warsaw and escape its brutal Second World War history in which the city rose up as the Red Army neared and was then razed by the Nazis. The Museum of the Warsaw Uprising at Ulica Grzybowska 79 (00 48 22 539 79 05; 1944.pl), which opened in 2004, uses video footage, photographs and various exhibits to explain how the tragic events of 1944 unfolded. It is open 10am to 6pm daily, until 8pm on Thursday and closed Tuesdays. Free entry on Sundays, otherwise 14 PLN (£2.80).

The icing on the cake

Take bus No 105 from outside the Museum to Foksal and change on to the E-2 bus to head out to the magnificent Baroque palace and park of Wilanow. Often called the Polish Versailles, about 10km south of the city centre. It opens 10.30am to 4pm Sunday, from 9.30am Wednesday to Saturday; closed Tuesdays; admission costs 20 PLN (£4).

PHOTO CAPTIONS AND COPYRIGHTS

ALSO AVAILABLE FROM THE INDEPENDENT

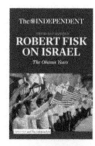

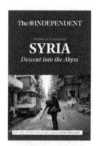

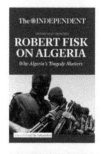

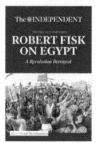

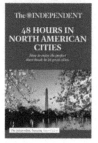

Lightning Source UK Ltd.
Milton Keynes UK
UKHW012346051218
333559UK00006B/536/P